In the Stillness Dancing

In the Stillness Dancing

The Journey of John Main

NEIL McKENTY

Darton, Longman and Todd
London

First published in 1986 by
Darton, Longman and Todd Ltd
89 Lillie Road, London SW6 1UD

Reprinted 1987

© 1986 Neil McKenty

ISBN 0 232 51709 6

British Library Cataloguing in Publication Data

McKenty, Neil
In the stillness dancing: the journey
of John Main.
1. Main, John, *d. 1982*   2. Benedictines—
Biography   3. Meditation
I. Title
248.3'4'0924   BX4705.M2631/

ISBN 0–232–51709–6

Phototypeset by Input Typesetting Ltd, London SW19 8DR
Printed and bound in Great Britain
Anchor Brendon Ltd, Tiptree

For Catharine

Contents

Illustrations

I said to my soul, be still, and wait without hope
For hope would be hope for the wrong thing; wait without
  love
For love would be love of the wrong thing; there is yet faith
But the faith and the love and the hope are all in the waiting.
Wait without thought, for you are not ready for thought:
So the darkness shall be the light, and the stillness the
  dancing.

T. S. Eliot, 'East Coker', Four Quartets.

Preface

I first met John Main on a sunny day in the early summer of 1979. He was sitting in a rickety chair on the veranda of the historic Décarie House in Notre-Dame-de-Grâce, a downtown suburb of Montreal. Dom (Father) John Main, a Benedictine monk for twenty years, was dressed casually in an open-necked white shirt, brown-coloured trousers and sandals. I had not anticipated so tall a man, above six feet, with the bearing of a member of the British army (which he had been) and the blue-eyed twinkle of an Irishman from Kerry (which he was).

A few months earlier I was talking with an old Jesuit friend. I told him I was successful in my work, radio broadcasting in Montreal, and happy in my marriage of seven years. Still, there was something missing. Both my wife, Catharine, and I had discussed this missing element and tried to put our finger on it. We could only agree that our lives, materially successful and happy, lacked a spiritual dimension. It was all we could think of to describe the sense of something lacking.

We both knew where to get a flat tyre fixed. But where do you go to get a spiritual dimension? The obvious answer was some religious group or institution. My wife was a Protestant. Her father had been a dedicated minister and missionary. For some years she had been associated with a Moral Re-Armament group, which she eventually left. She was wary of religious institutions and commitments. I shared her wariness.

For more than a quarter of a century I had been a member of the Jesuit Order. I had left in 1970 and I was not eager to join another organized religious enterprise. My wife and I went to Mass occasionally. But the service did not seem to mean much. So the vague feeling of something missing persisted. I mentioned my concern to my Jesuit friend. His response did not seem helpful: 'Have you ever heard of Father John Main?' I had not. 'Perhaps you should see him some time.'

I let the matter drop for several months. Then one day, I looked for John Main's name in the telephone directory and rang him up. The modulated voice that answered – was it British or Irish or both? – sounded warm and welcoming: 'By all means, come round this Sunday morning if you have time.'

So there we were sitting in the warm sun. John Main needed a larger house and he wanted to know about my raising money for Jesuit buildings. I also told him I had the devil of a time trying to pray as a Jesuit. I don't think he made any reply. In fact, I don't remember that we talked much about prayer at all.

I do remember asking him about the possibility of my wife and myself coming to the meditation groups he was instructing at the Priory he had founded after coming out from the Benedictine Abbey at Ealing in London in the autumn of 1977. John Main did not jump at the opportunity to sign up a high-profile prayer recruit from the world of the Montreal media. Instead, he said, 'I'll send you over some tapes I've made. Listen to them quietly, see what you think, then we'll have a chat again.' He sent the tapes, my wife and I listened and, eventually, what we heard changed our lives.

This did not happen overnight. Early in 1980 we both began to go to the Priory on Tuesday evenings. The procedure was simple. People sat quietly on more rickety furniture or on the floor, there was a little classical music, then John Main began to speak. He spoke with a penetrating authority that I had never heard before. When he spoke about love, as he often did, you felt he not only believed what he was saying about love – human and divine – but that he had experienced both, personally and profoundly. I remember too with what clarity he distinguished reality from illusion: how few pursued the real, how many the illusory. This was an aspect of his cosmic vision. For him it was incongruous not to be able to distinguish between reality and illusion. John Main was at his very best in these talks on meditation – authoritative, penetrating, persuasive.

In the few years I listened to John Main giving the Tuesday evening instruction on meditation and the homily at Sunday Mass (simple, scriptural, provocative), I never heard him utter a false note. There was wit and laughter, there was hyperbole and a delightful amount of verbal pyrotechnics and leg-pulling. There were points with which I disagreed. But never a false note.

The first time my wife and I spent a weekend at the Priory, I asked Father John whether he thought it would be a good idea if we tried to start a meditation group in our home. He thought it would. We did and it remains one of the richest experiences of our lives. One of the last times I saw Father John outdoors he came bounding down the monastery steps after the Tuesday night meditation to ask us how our meditation group was going.

The last time I was in his room at the Pine Avenue Priory, he was dying. During his life John Main gave many people a richer dimension for living. In his last hours he gave us an unforgettable perspective on dying. There was little sadness. Instead there was a sense permeating the monastery that a life had been waged and a victory was being won.

On the evening of the day he died, 30 December 1982, Father Laurence Freeman, his successor, asked me to write Dom John's biography. In doing our research, my wife, Catharine, and I have travelled to those places where John Main had so many friends and relatives – Dublin, Ballinskelligs, London, Washington. For us the pilgrimage of meditation, about which Dom John talked so often, has been a richer voyage than we ever imagined.

Once at his old monastery of Ealing, a close friend of John Main said to me at the end of our interview: 'John was a good man. He led people to God. Whatever you write, remember John was a good man.' *In The Stillness Dancing* is the journey of a modern monk and the story of a good man.

Perhaps the story of John Main osb would not have been published at all (certainly not now) without the co-operation of Father John's successor as Prior, Laurence Freeman osb.

It was his idea that a biography should be written. He discussed it with me and I agreed. Since I began the research in May 1983, in Ireland and England (with the help of my wife, Catharine), Father Laurence has been a tower of strength. He has given us material and insights from his long association with Father John. He has provided both encouragement and caution when these were required. He has never interfered with the integrity of the biography even when, I feel sure, he would have written a passage differently or omitted it altogether. Working with Father Laurence on Father John's biography has been an enriching part of our pilgrimage.

Other Benedictines who knew Father John have also helped in the project. I am indebted to Bernard Orchard OSB for arranging interviews for me at Ealing in London and to John Farrelly OSB for doing the same at St Anselm's in Washington. Michael Hall OSB provided me with some of Father John's key letters and he shared many of his own reminiscences.

I am also much indebted to the immediate members of Father John's family for making the research, especially in Ireland, not only more accurate but also more fun. I should mention Yvonne Fitzgerald, who shared her memories of her brother and arranged much of our Irish trip. Also her sisters, Diane O'Neill, and Kitty Stanley and her brother, Ian Main. In Dublin too, E. Y. Exshaw, Professor of Law at Trinity College, arranged interviews and made records available.

The help of Sister Madeleine Simon RSCJ, founder of the new Christian Meditation Centre in London, was indispensable. She interviewed Father John's associates, wrote letters, tracked down obscure records and provided me with much essential material. So, need I say, did Diana Ernaelsteen (Searle) whom Father John met when she was a little girl and considered a special friend all his life. Diana shared with me her memories and her letters and gave me the benefit of her perceptions and insights. I am also in the debt of Lady Lovat who made available many of the rich letters she received from Father John.

In Montreal two people, John Hallward and his wife, Clare, made a difference from the beginning. John's enthusiasm and advice made the book easier to do; Clare's encouragement and editing made it a better book. The suggestions of Sister Gertrude McLaughlin SNJM were invaluable. At the Montreal Priory, for help with preparing the manuscript, my thanks to Hélène Mercier, Doreen Romandini and Janet Johnson. My editor at Darton, Longman and Todd, Teresa de Bertodano, used the carrot far more often than the stick. Both were effective.

Finally, my wife Catharine, to whom the book is dedicated, supported the project with good humour and effective effort from beginning to end. She discovered material and people I never knew existed. We saw the book as a joint effort because we considered Father John a mutual friend to whom we both owed much. We did a lot of work but we also had a lot of fun. That seems appropriate for a book about John Main.

As these acknowledgements indicate, the material for the book came from many sources. The responsibility for the conclusions suggested in the book is mine alone.

Montreal   *Neil McKenty*

Introduction

The Journey Within

As the aircraft rolling down the runway of Washington's International Airport in the summer of 1974 gathered speed John Main should have been content. He had been a Benedictine monk for almost fifteen years. He was leaving Washington for London via Australia after four years as headmaster of St Anselm's private boys' school in the north-east section of the American capital. St Anselm's had prospered under his leadership and he had made many friends during his stay in Washington.

Still, as his aircraft climbed into the sky for the flight to San Francisco, John Main was not content. He was concerned. What he had observed during his five years in education in Washington had increased his concern about his Benedictine Order, the state of the Church, the effect of Christian education on young people, even the role of Christianity itself in the modern world. What John Main had detected in America was a malaise that none of the institutions he knew best were able to cope with. He described this concern to his old friends, the Akers-Jones, then in Hong Kong, with whom he had been associated in the British Oversea Civil Service in Malaya in the mid-1950s: 'The situation is so volatile you never know when it is going to blow up in your face. There is a tremendous amount of anxiety about and people live at the very edge of their nervous limit.'

It was the younger generation that concerned John Main for, despite his successful years as a headmaster in Washington, he questioned how well the staff at St Anselm's had prepared their students for life in the world: 'Would they know life in the dimension of spirit . . . or would their contact with life be restricted to the sense of a struggle for success?'

1

Why were so many younger people abandoning the institutional Church and seeking in the East what they could not
find in the West? Why did the journey East so often turn out
to be a spiritual cul-de-sac, just another ego-trip? Or as John
Main described it: '. . . we all know that the last ten or fifteen
years have shown that the search for experience out of context
only leads back deeper into the labyrinth of egoism'. Even
when people do not leave the institutional Church why do so
many merely use religion as an anaesthetic for their anxieties?
Why do so many others seek refuge in chemicals such as
drugs and alcohol?

'Is That All There Is?' was how a popular song tried to
capture the emptiness of materialism and success:

> What more and more of us are understanding in this world
> [he wrote] is that the human spirit cannot find fulfilment
> in mere material success or material prosperity. It isn't that
> material success or prosperity are bad in themselves but
> they are simply not adequate as a final, ultimate answer to
> the human situation.

Increasingly John Main saw 'the human situation' as one in
which men and women easily lost contact with reality, the
reality of themselves, the reality of the world around them.
Instead, illusions – marriage without love, work without
meaning, success without satisfaction – replaced reality or
were mistaken for it.

This phenomenon increasingly concerned John Main
during his years in Washington at the beginning of the
seventies. He suggested that most would not diagnose their
anxiety as a loss of 'essential harmony, awareness, consciousness or spirit'. Instead, he says:

> We would be much more likely to point to particular
> features of our life such as work, relationships, health, and
> to attribute our unhappiness or anxiety to one or all of
> these. Many people, indeed, would not even see all these
> different aspects of their life as having any common point
> of contact. . . . The result of this is that modern life so often
> lacks a centre, a point of convergence, a source of unity.

The longer he lived, the more John Main saw lives that were

fragmented, shallow and that lacked a spiritual dimension. And the longer he lived, the more determined he became to confront this tragedy.

By the time he left Washington to return to London in the summer of 1974, Dom John Main had concluded that organized religion was not adequately coping with the anxieties and frustration of the human situation. Some years later he underlined this inadequacy:

> Out of every area of Christian thought and activity today there comes the same insistence that abstract or legalistic answers to the riddles of our lives are inadequate. Rulebook regulations applied without human compassion for the uniqueness of each individual are as futile as the neat intellectual formulas that have no integral power to change the way we live.

This became the fundamental question that lay at the base of John Main's future work. Indeed it formed the basis for his own spiritual journey, 'What is the power to change the way we live and how do we make contact with that power?' At the heart of this question, for John Main, lay the failure of the Church: 'As if a city without electricity was lighting its streets with candles while a great power source lay untapped. . . .' People turned elsewhere.

Yet John Main became convinced that people, far from discarding real religious truth, were more thirsty for it than ever:

> There is a great feeling among our contemporaries, I think, of the need, perhaps even the extreme urgent need to recover the spiritual dimension of our lives. There is a feeling that unless we do recover that spiritual dimension we are going to lose our grip on life altogether.

At the same time John Main was no kill-joy. A commitment to spiritual values, far from being a rejection of the daily joys of living, led him to a deeper enthusiasm for life. He had friends all over the world. He had an intense appreciation for good music, good books, the beauty of a flower, the expanse of the sea. John Main believed those who embarked on a voyage of discovery to live life in the deep led, even at the human level, a more exciting life than those who lived in the shallows.

But how to recover this dimension now that the old formulas, the trite answers no longer sufficed? Wherever John Main travelled he sensed this search for a spiritual dimension, for a relationship with God that was not itself an illusion but real. But how? John Main was beginning to formulate a way:

> It seemed to me that the generalities with which people had been conditioned no longer satisfied them. The search for God, for absolute value and personal meaning, was a search for a way to pray, to find God in self and self in God and, above all, to find a way that was possible for modern men and women.

And again:

> All of us feel . . . a need to find something, some principle in our lives that is absolutely reliable and worthy of our confidence. All of us feel this impulse to somehow or other make contact with rock-like reality.

But again the practical question. How do we move from the shallows to the deep? How do we harmonize and unify a life that has been split and fragmented so long? John Main put the problem this way:

> The question . . . which is asked by all modern men and women and not just by religious people is: 'How can we get back into touch with ourselves? How do we recover a sense of confidence in ourselves, the confidence of knowing that we really do exist in our own right?'

How then do people whose lives have been largely directed by others, whose expectations and goals are determined externally, who feel frustrated and fragmented – how do they turn their lives around?

John Main describes this alienation in *Moment of Christ*: 'I think people suffer a great deal of frustration because they cannot be themselves and cannot make contact with themselves. James Joyce once described one of his characters as "always living at a certain distance from himself".' How is it possible to reduce this crippling gap between what we appear to be (especially to others) and what we were meant to be? Is there a way to our own centre where we can simply *be* – where we don't need to justify ourselves or apologize for ourselves but where we simply rejoice in the gift of being ourselves?

The answer to that question depends on a closer analysis of the problem. John Main goes to its root this way:

> The great illusion that most of us are caught in is that we are the centre of the world and everything and everyone revolves around us. . . . This is a very easy illusion to fall into because in the opening consciousness of life it seems that we are understanding the external world from our own centre. And we seem to be monitoring the outside world from an interior control centre. And so it seems as though the world is revolving around us. Then logically we begin to try to control that world, to dominate it and to put it at our service. This is the way to alienation, to loneliness, to anxiety because it is fundamentally unreal.

How does one move away from alienation, anxiety and loneliness? Is there a bridge from illusion and the unreal to the real? How does one turn from the periphery to find the centre? In a word how does one begin 'the journey within'?

For John Main 'the journey within' began on the outskirts of Kuala Lumpur, a Malayan city in the spring of 1955. There John Main, newly graduated from Law at Trinity College, Dublin, was assigned to study language in the British Oversea Civil Service. And there, in sight of the Malayan jungle, he happened to meet a Hindu swami at his school and meditation centre. The two talked about prayer and meditation. John Main began to meditate using a short Christian prayer phrase now commonly called a mantra. Some years later the meeting with the Hindu swami led John Main to discover another meditator. His name was John Cassian. He was a Christian monk who lived in the desert near Cairo in the fourth century. He also used a short prayer phrase or mantra.

It was not until twenty years after he met the Hindu swami that John Main fully realized the power of Christian meditation to change the way we live – in our homes, in our churches, in our world. He began in the summer of 1975 by forming a small prayer group at his Benedictine monastery at Ealing in London. The effect was like tossing a pebble into a deep pool. It scarcely broke the surface. Only later would the ripples spread across Britain and Ireland and the oceans to the world. From the beginning John Main considered it absolutely necessary to meditate together in silence with those who came to the first groups at Ealing. And he followed this practice for the rest of his life. But gradually, from the experience of the silent prayer itself, John Main began to ponder and reflect, then to write about the tradition and the process of Christian meditation. Several themes developed: prayer is a journey to the God dwelling within, rooted in St Paul's teaching, 'the secret of Christ in you'. This journey within requires silence (the active, concentrated silence of a watchmaker poised over his watch). This journey to the centre avoids thoughts and images about God. How can an infinite God be circumscribed by human thoughts and imaginings? John Main, always wary of the potential words have to distort, tried to find the words to describe Christian meditation:

> To meditate means to live out of the centre of our being, that profound centre we find when we determine not to be shallow, not to be content to rest on the surface, to live out of the depths of our being.

The greatest obstacle to the journey within, to living from our own depths, is our preoccupation with ourselves, our self-centredness:

> Self-consciousness is like having a mirror between ourselves and God. Every time we look into the mirror we see ourselves. The purpose of meditation is to smash that mirror so that we no longer look at reflections of things and consequently see everything backwards, including ourselves. . . . Perhaps that is what brings most of us to meditation. We don't want to look into that mirror and see everything backwards for the rest of our lives. We want to look through it, beyond it, and beyond ourselves.

Why do most people begin to meditate? Why did the meditation groups at Ealing expand so rapidly? John Main's speculation on this question has profound implications for the modern Church:

> What we began to see more sharply was that [the spiritual crisis of our times] was not just a crisis of materialism, of a loss of spiritual values. . . . The crisis was the men and women of deep spiritual seriousness and hunger who were being denied the vital reference points of their growth to maturity and who lacked the personal communication of teaching authority and experience – it was these who were really in crisis. . . . These were the real apostles on whom the building up of the Body [of Christ] depended. . . . And if these ordinary people living and working in the world lacked the transforming experience in their own hearts, where would be their power to transform their world in love?

Why did these ordinary people, living and working in the world, come to the prayer groups at Ealing? 'They came to us for the most part because they felt they did lack it [i.e. the transforming experience], though exactly what "it" was they would not all perhaps have been able to say.' All these ordinary people knew was they had asked for bread and received a stone. In *Letters from the Heart* John Main writes that those who came to Ealing 'knew, often in a very simple faith trained in the old ways, that ritual obedience and personal devotions could not of themselves be the gospel experience. They felt the void but were no longer content to try to fill it with religious distraction.' On the contrary, quite the opposite was the case:

> The lay people who came were in serious and profound search for a way to enter into the direct and personal experience of God and, if they were Christians, they believed that this meant the way of prayer – a prayer that could no longer be defined as talking to God, but a prayer that could only be described as their awareness of God in Jesus.

In the words of one of John Main's favourite writers, Cardinal Newman, a 'notional assent' to dogma and ritual was no longer adequate. People were seeking a real participation in the experience of the Risen Jesus.

The way to this experience was through prayer. Nothing John Main said at Ealing or later provoked more difficulty than his words on prayer. Most people in the Christian tradition have been taught vocal prayer, usually a prayer of petition. If they had been introduced to mental prayer at all, chances are it was a kind of mental prayer teeming with inner words, images, thoughts and speculations. Like the world we live in, it was a busy kind of prayer. It was not the prayer Dom John spoke about: 'We are all basically aware that we cannot apprehend God by thinking about him.' If God cannot be grasped in thought (like a proposition of Pythagoras or Einstein or Lonergan) how can he be experienced? John Main answers in *Letters from the Heart*:

> The God who cannot be thought of or imagined can be known in love. . . . So often when we talk to God we are talking about ourselves . . . the structure of the words keeps us at the centre of our own consciousness. . . . In meditation God the unknowable is at the centre. And as we move steadily into union with that centre, we come to know him by his own light – always a progressive loss of self and self-consciousness. . . . The attempt to imagine God or Jesus is as fruitless an exercise at the time of prayer as talking to him or theologizing about him. We imagine only those who are absent.

Often when speaking of 'imageless' prayer John Main returns to the image of human love. He had experienced human love in the warmth of his family and as a student at Trinity College, Dublin. He did not just think about love, or imagine love or express it in words; he shared the experience, often in silence. As with human love, so with divine. For John Main it was not enough to develop images about love or speculate about it or discuss it even with the beloved. Love must be shared and experienced, at its deepest level, in silence.

Still, if prayer is not an internal dialogue (or monologue) with God, what is it? In the summer of 1976, John Main tried to answer that question put to him by the Trappists at

Gethsemani Abbey in Kentucky, for so long the home of Thomas Merton:

> ... all Christian prayer [he said] is a growing awareness of God in Jesus. . . . And for that growing awareness we need to come to a state of undistraction, to a state of attention and concentration – that is to a state of awareness . . . the only way that I have been able to find to come to that quiet, to that undistractedness, is the way of the mantra.

Twenty years before, John Main had been initiated into the way of the mantra by the Hindu swami. Gradually, the way of the mantra became the vehicle of John Main's own prayer. He usually recommended the prayer phrase or mantra, 'Maranatha', an ancient Aramaic prayer, 'Come Lord'. The reasons for repeating the mantra quietly and unceasingly, during the time of meditation were two: to wean the mind from thinking about its own pre-occupations and to induce an interior silence that was the predisposition for God's action, in faith, at the deepest centre.

John Main described the function of the mantra or prayer phrase in many ways, including some derived from his days with Army Intelligence in the Second World War:

> The mantra . . . is like a harmonic that we sound in the depths of our spirit, bringing us to an ever-deepening sense of our own wholeness and central harmony. It leads us to the source of this harmony, to our centre, rather as a radar bleep leads an aircraft home through thick fog. It also rearranges us, in the sense that it brings all our powers and faculties into line with each other just as a magnet drawn over iron filings pulls them into their proper force fields.

But he insisted the mantra was not some verbal abracadabra:

> As you all know from your own experience the mantra is not magic. It is not an incantation, and learning to say your mantra means learning to follow a way of life in which *everything* in your life is attuned to God. And so, in a sense, everything in your life is attuned to the mantra.

And the mantra, he sometimes said, is not taught, it's caught.

Obviously John Main was sensitive to the suggestion (sometimes the accusation) that he was promoting some new-fangled 'imageless' prayer based on a mantra imported from some exotic land. What was this so-called Christian meditation if so many people had never heard of it, let alone practised it? Actually the tradition of mantric prayer has been around a long time. It was implicit in the ancient Jewish custom of 'blessing the Lord at all times'. Perhaps it was also veiled in the rhythmic Aramaic phrases of the Lord's Prayer. A prayer phrase or mantra was explicitly used in the Orthodox Churches in the well-known words of the 'Jesus Prayer' ('Lord, be merciful to me, a sinner'). The use of a single prayer phrase first entered the West through a monk (and a teacher of St Benedict himself), John Cassian, toward the end of the fourth century. Cassian received the mantra from the desert fathers who placed its origins in Apostolic times. Much later, in the fourteenth century, the anonymous author of the spiritual classic, *The Cloud of Unknowing*, urged serious meditators to relinquish thoughts and images and to 'pray not in many words but in a little word of one syllable'.

Nor did John Main have much patience with those who argued that 'imageless' prayer was only for the select few. His prime witness for the opposite view is St Paul. Paul urges his readers – without exception – to unceasing prayer at the same time that he tells them they don't know how to pray. For St Paul, as for John Main, there was only one prayer. It was the unceasing prayer of Jesus to his Father made present in every human heart by the Holy Spirit. The task of the meditator was not to construct some other prayer but to become present, in faith, to the prayer of Jesus to the Father. The first step is to begin, by an act of faith, the journey within. Then, turning away from the consciousness of self with the help of the mantra, the meditator develops in faith a growing presence to the prayer of Jesus to his Father. Was this prayer for the experts only, the elite religious in monasteries? Not according to St Paul and not according to John Main.

There were several views on prayer that raised John Main's Irish hackles. One was the suggestion that Christian meditation was only for the illuminati staring into the wild blue yonder from their cloistered gardens. In *Word Into Silence* when he was describing the need for stillness and concentration as conditions to dispose the meditator to participate, in faith, in the prayer of Jesus to his Father, John Main wrote: 'Now many Christians would still say at this point, "Very well, but this is for Saints, for specialists in prayer," as if stillness and silence were not universal elements of the human spirit.' John Main gave this objection short shrift: 'This type of obstinate false humility is based on a plain unawareness of who St Paul was writing to in Rome and Corinth and Ephesus. He was not writing to specialists, to Carmelites and Carthusians, but to husbands, wives, butchers and bakers.'

Nor was John Main talking to specialists in prayer. He was talking to labourers, to people who worked the night shift, nurses, teachers, professionals, families with children. He often said little children caught on quickest to what he was talking about, being present to God through faith in prayer.

About twenty centuries after Paul's letters on unceasing prayer for all, a famous monk modified his views about the accessibility of meditation. Originally Thomas Merton considered meditation or contemplation so difficult few would ever progress in it. Merton thought the practice of contemplation, the simple prayer of presence, should be restricted to the professed religious in contemplative orders. Later in his published works Merton qualified his position. He raised the possibility of meditation being available for everyone. Merton had come to see that contemplation was not a professional exercise for professionals. Instead Merton realized that mental prayer was a personal experience to be authenticated.

Thomas Merton's biographer describes his changed views on prayer this way:

> . . . He saw now that, definitions apart, contemplation could only be made real to others when it was demonstrated in a life. Contemplation and living drew closer together. It was more urgent than ever to free both of self-awareness. . . . He saw more and more clearly that it was the *lived* life, not the written life, that should be contemplative. . . . Out of prayerful meditation upon

11

emptiness would come a sense of intimate relationship with God, a God free of the limits of concept.

To be free of self-awareness and to be present in faith to 'a God free of the limits of concept' were words that John Main might have written. As for Merton he was using the 'Jesus Prayer' eleven years before his death. At the beginning of 1966, Merton, who seldom described his own prayer, wrote to an Eastern friend:

> Strictly speaking I have a very simple way of prayer. It is centred entirely on attention to the presence of God. . . . Yet it does not mean imagining anything or conceiving a precise image of God, for to my mind that would be a kind of idolatry. . . . It is not 'thinking about' anything, but a direct seeking of the Face of the Invisible.

Still later, by 1968, according to his biographer, 'Thomas Merton had become an existential contemplative. This meant only that he had discovered the authentic journey and much of it would have to be made in silence.' And so, near the end, Merton was moving in the spirit of his prayer to his patroness, Our Lady of Carmel, 'Teach me to go to the country beyond words and beyond names.' In Ealing in 1975 John Main's prayer groups were in 'the country beyond words and beyond names'.

In the autumn of 1977, at the invitation of Bishop Leonard Crowley, Dom John Main and a Benedictine associate, Laurence Freeman, left Ealing to establish a monastery in Montreal. Soon would-be meditators from a broad spectrum – store clerks, professors, businessmen, students, artists – came to the monastery in an old historic house in an inner suburb of Montreal. So strong was the response that in two years the monastery moved to more spacious quarters, an estate in the city's centre on the slopes of Mount Royal Park overlooking Montreal and the St Lawrence River.

Dom John Main did not fear that city life need distort monastic values. Rather he felt urban pressures would simplify monastic life: 'This was so because the world, in a small way, was coming to us, and its mobility, joined creatively with our stability, was to form a new kind of cloister

. . . with a spiritual continuum below the world's restlessness.'
John Main saw the monastery and the prayer groups as vital
spiritual cells of stability and simplicity:

> There is no way any society can achieve internal harmony
> or belief in its own meaning without such centres of spiri-
> tual simplicity and commitment operating in peace and
> seriousness out of resources that are beyond social
> control. . . . More and more the monastery will fulfil its
> prophetic role by living in the cities where the experience
> of community and spirit are all but lost. There, in these
> modern deserts, it will bloom by the proof of the power of
> faith and absolute generosity to achieve the impossible in
> liberty of spirit.

By the autumn of 1982 prayer groups had formed in
Montreal and Quebec, spread through the other provinces of
Canada, in Europe, Africa and South America, in the United
States and in England and Ireland which Dom John tried to
visit each summer. Thousands of other people (many of whom
would never meet John Main) had become serious twice-daily
meditators by listening to his tapes and reading his books
such as *Word Into Silence* and *Letters from the Heart.*
These prayer groups and their meditators were a cross
section of the population. Some were Christians; others were
not. Some Catholics; others not. An Anglican bishop from
Ontario meditated. So did students of Eastern religion. A
journalist covering the carnage in Beirut meditated when he
could. So did a woman doctor, a member of the Irish Medical
Missionaries of Mary, who was attached to a nomadic tribe
in Africa. A Sanskrit scholar meditates with her husband in
London. A meditator, originally from Holland, organized a
weekly meditation group for senior citizens in Montreal. A
woman musician and a bio-chemist lead a group in New
Zealand. A Protestant Minister and his wife formed a group
in New York City, as did a writer and his wife, the manager
of an art gallery, in Boston. And so it goes on, an actor in
London, an English professor at Harvard, a radio broadcaster
in Montreal, a nun working with orphans in Honduras, a
founder of Alcoholics Anonymous in Canada, a student of

physics at the Massachusetts Institute of Technology, an editor in New York, a calligrapher and a violinist in Montreal.

Father John tried to keep in touch with all the meditators through a newsletter he wrote, which was published about four times yearly at the Montreal monastery. In these letters he never minced words about the efficacy of the prayer-tradition he lived by and wrote about. If some objected to the claims he made for Christian meditation, Dom John did not then dilute the teaching: 'If I seem to be intolerant of other ways it is not because I wish to dismiss other ways or traditions. It is only because the faith I have in this monastic way and tradition is a loving and urgent one.'

Urgent. It was an apt word to describe Father John's later years. He had always seen the basic Christian paradox as the losing of one's life to find it. It is impossible to resolve a paradox. One can only transcend it – through the power of love at the human level, through meditation at the divine. In speaking of this – losing one's life to find it, transcendence, the power of love – Father John wrote to all the meditators, 'I feel a great sense of urgency to share this with all of you.' This sense of urgency became more acute after the autumn of 1979. At that time the doctors operated on Father John for cancer. The operation appeared to be successful. But the cancer reappeared. In the summer of 1982, John Main was getting about his monastery in a wheel chair. The cancer was spreading rapidly.

About five months after John Main's death, on 30 December 1982, a meditator wrote about his future biography:

Sometimes I felt he was so far ahead that it was discouraging for those of us who were still struggling at a lower stage. Often I felt I would have preferred his letters if he would say something of the struggle – his struggle which he must have experienced from time to time. I guess what I am trying to say . . . is that I hope . . . you can present not just the finished product, as it were, but something of the man and his struggles.

For example, in my last talk with him, I said it must be very difficult on the one hand to have people who adored

14

him and, on the other, a constant battle with pain. To which he replied, 'It is all in the Lord.'

I think I know what he meant but it is a high stage of spiritual development and I would like to know more about how he got there.

In the Stillness Dancing is about the man and his struggles and something of how he got there.

1

Beginnings in Ballinskelligs

On a February night in 1960 a Benedictine monk from Ealing Abbey in a suburb of London dropped by the Chelsea flat of an old Trinity College friend. He stayed just long enough to change from his habit into evening dress. Then John Main left for the festivities at Gray's Inn where he had been called to the Bar, the first English monk so honoured since the Reformation.

Who was this slim, tall young man just turned thirty-four, with his sandy hair and piercing blue eyes who moved so easily from the spiritual world of Ealing to the secular temples of the courts? Why had he left a promising career in the law, a closely-knit family in Ireland and the young woman he loved, to become a Benedictine monk? How was it that John Main became so excited by the prayer life of a Christian writer who lived in the desert in the fourth century and to whom he was led by a Hindu swami?

Why would the prior of an established monastery in London later give it all up to go off and set up shop in an old house in Montreal, Quebec? And how was it so many people, seeking a new dimension in their lives, journeyed to the priory he founded in Montreal, discovered John Main and were forever changed by the discovery? The answer lay in John Main's own journey.

The journey began at 12 Egerton Gardens, Hendon in London where he was born on 21 January 1926. His father, David Patrick Main, had been born in 1893 in Ballinskelligs, County Kerry, on the southern coast of Ireland where he worked as a 'cable telegraphist' for the Western Union Company. His grandfather, also David Patrick, had arrived from Scotland to become superintendent of the first trans-

16

atlantic cable station established near Ballinskelligs in 1866. After he retired from the cable station John Main's grandfather helped build a hotel, called Main's Hotel. For many years, Main was the important name in Ballinskelligs. Besides the hotel the Mains ran a grocery store, a post office, a fleet of boats and chauffeured cars for the tourists. Unhappily for his own fortunes, Main's Hotel was not left to John's father but to an older brother.

His mother, Eileen Hurley, born in Moat, County Meath in 1887, was six years older than her future husband, David Main. It was through his mother that he acquired a famous ancestor, the Irish nationalist, author and journalist, Charles J. Kickham, born in 1828. A description of Kickham fits his descendant: 'keen, piercing eyes, which had a strange power of reading one's very thought. . . .' In his most popular novel, *Knocknagow*, written a year before his death in 1882, Charles Kickham wrote: 'Glory to God in the highest and on earth enthusiasm.' It was an epitaph that described the lives of Eileen Hurley and her son.

After her education in Moat, Eileen went to Belgium for finishing school and later became a nurse. It was as a nurse that she, then 32, first met her future husband. In 1919 David Main, aged 26, was in bed with influenza. Eileen had gone to Ballinskelligs to help in the influenza epidemic. She was small, blondish, pretty and refined. Almost immediately David Main fell in love with his new nurse. But there was a problem. Eileen Hurley was engaged to another man. David said that would not make any difference. And it did not. David simply told Eileen to break her engagement. He even suggested that she do this at the Metropole Hotel in Cork and he went along to make certain there were no slip-ups. There were none.

Then David took his bride-to-be to Roach's jewellery store to purchase an engagement ring. 'Mickey' Roach was astonished to see Eileen accept a second ring from another man. But David Main was never one to waste time. He and Eileen Hurley, the future parents of six children, were married at St Peter and St Paul's Church in the city of Cork on 7 February 1920. After their marriage David and Eileen spent only a short time in Ballinskelligs where, as the mountains of Kerry slope into the sea, the Skelligs Rocks rise off the shore, the site of one of the most spectacular and ancient monastic communities in Europe, a community that would exert an influence on John Main's life. Then, in the early 1920s after the birth of their first daughter Kitty, on 10 November 1920, Western Union transferred David Main from Ballinskelligs to London.

During their first three years in London, David and Eileen had two more children, Ian in 1922 and Yvonne in 1924. Then came Douglas, with a quick and easy birth, on 21 January 1926. Ten days later he was baptized Douglas William Victor at Our Lady of Sorrows, Egerton Gardens, Hendon, the Main's parish church. William and Victor were after his two uncles, his father's brothers. But where did 'Douglas' come from? Apparently his Aunt Ethel, his father's sister, was reading a book whose protagonist was called 'Douglas'. When the baby was born earlier than expected Aunt Ethel cast about for a third name. So Douglas William Victor it was (the name John only when he became a monk). After Douglas in 1926, came two more children, Diane two years later and Allan Patrick in 1929.

A new city, another position with Western Union and six children in the space of nine years meant a bustling Main household. David Main was a strong disciplinarian with an explosive temper that sometimes frightened his children. He was a man's man with an eye for pretty women. He would waltz into the Main's post office at Ballinskelligs, singing 'Home Sweet Home' at the top of his fine musical voice, and kiss the first good-looking young woman he saw. Then he would go home and tell Eileen all about it.

David Main was a man whom most men liked and most women found attractive. He played tennis, golf and billiards and, despite a slight limp, he was usually dressed to the nines and cut a dapper figure about London, Belfast, and later Dublin. He never allowed the mundane to interfere with his polished appearance. If Eileen wanted a pound of sausages, David had them carefully wrapped, not in a greasy brown bag, but inside his gleaming brief-case. When he travelled he sold Irish sweep tickets on the side. His family was never in want but money was sometimes scarce. Despite the fact he was in some ways unpredictable and quick-tempered, David Main loved his family. They loved him and they shared fun together. Every summer there was a family holiday. Once David hired a man and his lorry to transport the Main family, all eight of them, around Sussex. This time the lorry was parked near a travelling circus. Perhaps intrigued by the Main menagerie, a giraffe stuck its head into the back of the lorry. Whereupon David Main instructed the lorry driver to avoid the police at all costs lest the whole kit and caboodle be charged with running an over-loaded and illegal transport service.

David Main was a born actor. Once his constituency Member of Parliament was making a speech filled with the usual political clichés. At the end of the speech, David Main jumped up and demanded a 'Yes' or 'No' answer to a very convoluted question. The puzzled parliamentarian confessed, 'I'm afraid I don't understand the question.' Whereupon Main stood up again to accuse the poor man of stonewalling. The crowd burst into laughter and cheers. David Main had turned a dull evening into an exciting event. It was a lesson Douglas learned well: to make an adventure from the humdrum. On another occasion in his own drawing room in London, David interrupted a discussion on George Bernard Shaw, about whom he knew little, with the remark, 'Ah yes, Shaw. Of course, he was quite an unknown quantity, you know.' The guests, some of whom knew a lot about Shaw, were stunned. But Douglas who was present saw the moral of the story at once. Lack of knowledge was not fatal. Self-confidence was the thing. Later Douglas, who once described his father as 'a wild Irishman with a mop of black curly hair', would often use self-confidence and braggadocio to highlight a humorous situation.

There's no doubt David Main had self-confidence to burn. He burned it selling sweepstake tickets (typically he gave that up once they were legalized), he burned it at the race-track and he burned it in shaky business transactions. As a respite from these and the constrictions of raising a large family on modest resources, David Main liked nothing better than to get back to Ballinskelligs (a liking not shared by his wife) and chew over the local news in Gaelic with his buddies in

Kerry. The stories and the Irish whiskey were a potent brew for the 'schanachies' (Irish story-tellers) as they spun their tales around the bar of Main's Hotel in Ballinskelligs. In another emanation David Main would have made a splendid character actor (as indeed would his son, Douglas). As a family man, however, David, in some ways, was 'a street angel and a house divil'.

Whatever the hullabaloo, Eileen Hurley Main never seemed to lose her composure. She was quiet, gentle and very Irish. She shared with her husband a strong Catholic faith. In religious practice, however, Eileen never insisted on the letter of the law, for example, not eating meat on Friday if the meat would then go bad. Eileen said God was more concerned with the waste than he was with the rule. She worried about people down on their luck. She called them 'waifs and strays' and more often than not (usually after a telephone call from the local parish priest) Eileen would invite a 'waif' or a 'stray' in for a meal, maybe to stay the night or longer.

There was the time the wife of an official of the famous Raffle's Hotel in Singapore showed up on her door step in London. Eileen knew the woman had a drinking problem. She invited her in, gave her a good meal, then ensconced her in the master Main bedroom for the night. Sometime after midnight David Main arrived home unexpectedly. Naturally thinking he would find his wife in bed he bustled into the master-bedroom, threw back the covers and discovered instead the wife of an official of Raffle's Hotel. 'My God, woman, what are you doing?' he shrieked. Eileen merely laughed. 'When you have a guest in the house,' she said, 'you give the guest nothing but the best.' It was a custom Douglas never forgot.

David Main usually knew better than to argue with his wife. Later Douglas would call his mother 'the gentle persuader'. She normally got her way without losing her temper. She was easy-going, more reticent than the Mains, sometimes living in a kind of dream world. When one of her children said, 'I'd like to dye my hair,' Eileen did not say 'No!!' She asked, 'What colour?' When the children played hide-and-seek it didn't fuss her to find one in her laundry hamper. She just put the lid back down. Sunday night was family night at the Main household, not just for the Mains but for half the families in the neighbourhood. David Main had a fine singing voice. He wanted everybody to sing. What's more he ordered them to. There were games. People wrote down a subject for a one-minute speech. Then the topics were drawn from a hat. Douglas' older brother, Ian, was outraged when he drew the topic suggested by Douglas, 'Early Byzantine Architecture'. Even at this time, aged seven or eight, no one was quite certain how seriously to take Douglas. Throughout his life, Douglas had fun with exaggeration and hyperbole. His sisters and surviving brother still remember, aghast, 'the lies he used to tell'.

There was a mischievous side to Douglas. Once he and a group of his friends visited a local cemetery. Douglas noticed that some graves had flowers, others did not. He suggested they redistribute all the flowers. They did. Playing 'doctors and nurses' with his older sister, Yvonne, about to have her leg 'amputated', Douglas would say, 'Don't worry, Madame, this knife is quite blunt.' Sometimes Douglas would entertain guests while his mother made tea. Once he startled a north London matron by asking, 'What do you think of the Abyssinian question?' From his parents' marriage, not romantic, volatile at times, but built on a solid bond between two complementary personalities, Douglas first experienced the warmth of human love.

But even in these early years there was another side to Douglas: quiet, shy, introspective and religious. From his father, accurate and pragmatic, Douglas acquired his precision. From his mother, spiritual, more of a dreamer, Douglas gained his insight into religious values and his imaginative flair. From the beginning there was a strong bond between Douglas and Eileen. She had immense influence on his spiritual pilgrimage. He was proud of his mother. Much later he would join clubs in various cities. One of the reasons was so that he could take Eileen dining in style.

Others noticed this close bond between Douglas and Eileen and also his quiet, reflective side. An older relative described Douglas at seven or eight:

He was, I thought, a very quiet and serious little lad but he always seemed to be making a study of people. Maybe this is why he was such a good mimic. . . . Maybe his appearance as a serious child was all part of the act. . . . Douglas was always a popular child and very much so with adults. This again, I think, is because he made a great study of all.

There was also a steady religious influence in the Main home. Naturally, in a Roman Catholic family then, there was regular Mass on Sunday and prayers in the evening. The Main children, like children in many Christian homes, played 'religious' games. Douglas and his brother, Ian, often played a game called 'Bishops'. Although Ian was older, invariably Douglas was the bishop and Ian his assistant. Somewhat indecorously, the altar bell was sounded on a chamber pot. Douglas used to dress up as a priest with a dash of red to denote ecclesiastical rank. He made an 'altar' in his bedroom and his sisters were dragooned into 'serving Mass'.

Many years later a boyhood friend saw these early religious 'games' as the real beginning of Douglas Main's spiritual journey:

When he eventually made the break and went to Canada to concentrate on his meditative studies, one or two people said to me rather unkindly: 'Typical Douglas – I always knew he would start a new religion.' To me it was only the logical outcome of that facet of his character and forming inner self that I had seen so vividly in childhood. . . . Early in his life I was privileged to see on an intimate basis what was later to develop so strongly. He never really changed. From his childhood his later life was inevitable.

2

From Circus Master to the Jesuits

The important people of Hendon were in their places, the borough's councillors looked suitably interested, and the school hall was packed with proud parents, including David and Eileen Main. Suddenly the calliope music began, the curtains parted and 'The Circus', the Christmas play for 1931 at St Mary's parochial school in Hendon, was about to start. The circus master, Douglas Main, five years old, confidently walked on stage. The audience clapped, Douglas bowed, and the show began. Douglas' first teacher, Grace Ward, had chosen him to be circus master. She had sized him up that autumn in the reception class at St Mary's. She was sure he would acquit himself well.

Now he stood on the stage resplendent in a black top hat, a little velvet jacket, long trousers and white gloves. But the *pièce de résistance* was the long snaky black whip. When Douglas cracked his whip the make-believe elephants rumbled past, the little girls dressed like fairies cowered in mock fear, the 'funny horse' bowed stiff-jointedly to the audience. Douglas Main gave his whip several more snaps and cracks. He loved it. So did the audience as Douglas, holding his top hat in his hand, bowed in turn to the 'funny horse'.

The play was a great success. Grace Ward had chosen Douglas to be circus master because of his natural poise, unusual in a boy aged only five. As she says: 'His whole life and soul was in it. He was marvellous. He became the circus master.' This was the first time Douglas Main acted a role in the world of make-believe in public. Later on it would sometimes be difficult to distinguish the role Douglas Main was playing from the reality.

In the class-room itself, Douglas began his career as a good average student. What impressed Grace Ward, besides his easy poise, was how well he got on with a mixed group of children. During his first year in elementary school Douglas Main also struck his teacher as refined, self-possessed and, although not overly robust, not delicate either. In fact, there was some concern in the Main household about Douglas's health. Both he and his older sister, Yvonne, were subject to ear infections. His parents decided a stint in the country air would not hurt Douglas and would build him up physically. So in the early spring of 1932, they packed him off to Ballinskelligs to stay with his Uncle William (his father's older brother) and his Aunt Nell. Early in March Douglas began classes in the local national school where John O'Sullivan was headmaster (known as John the Master, to distinguish him from all the other O'Sullivans in county Kerry) and where his teacher was Sean O'Connor, a powerful Gaelic football player whom Douglas grew to worship.

Usually it is not easy to begin school part-way through the year. This might be one reason Douglas Main did not much like going to school at Ballinskelligs. Another might be the attitude of some of the older boys. They considered Douglas, with his English accent and mannerisms, a bit of a 'swell' from London. Whatever the reasons for his dislike of school, Douglas managed to get into his share of mischief during the few weeks he spent in Ballinskelligs. To get out of school altogether he would tell his Aunt Nell at breakfast that he was not feeling well. Naturally this did not impress Aunt Nell, so off he went. On one occasion he asked Aunt Nell what it was like over on Horse Island just off the coast near Ballinskelligs. Unknown to his unsuspecting Aunt, Douglas knew all about what it was like on Horse Island. He had talked one of the local fishermen into taking him there in his boat.

Although this was the beginning of his life-long fondness for Ballinskelligs and County Kerry, it is unlikely Douglas then visited the area's most famous site, the Skelligs Rocks, rocky Islands about eight miles from the mainland. The most spectacular is the Great Skellig (or Skellig Michael) rising more than 700 feet above the stormy Atlantic. A Christian monastic movement, originating in Egypt in the fourth century, was responsible for monastic hermitages developing near the summit of the Great Skellig at the end of the sixth century. These hermitages continued to exist there for the next 600 years. When he later visited this sacred spot, Douglas Main, like others, felt a sense of direct contact with the earliest life of Irish Christianity and monasticism. Is there any doubt these monastic foundations (later moved into Ballinskelligs itself), influenced Douglas's own pilgrimage? As one of his close associates said, 'Ballinskelligs was always with him'.

In any event, Douglas returned to St Mary's School in Hendon in time to make his first Holy Communion. The school was proud of its emphasis on religious practice and knowledge. Grace Ward found her young charges eager to learn the catechism, and she taught them prayers by memory. There were dramatized stories from the Bible, a favourite part of the children's school day. Probably Sister Campion, another excellent teacher, prepared Douglas for his first Communion about the time of the feast of Corpus Christi in the late spring of 1932.

Douglas's next experience of school was not so happy. By this time, 1934, his parents had moved to a larger house at 108 Muswell Hill Road in north London. There was no Catholic school in the area so Douglas and his older brother, Ian, went to the Highgate Junior School in North Hill, Highgate. He entered the school on 10 April 1934. He did not like the school nor did he get on well with the other boys (although Ian seems to have had no trouble). Douglas considered the other boys to be rough and they looked on him as a snob and a 'toff'. However, he did well enough academically especially in his religious classes; he shared top honours with a girl in Scripture studies. Another girl who sat at the desk in front of him at Highgate Junior School remembers Douglas this way: 'He was a very religious boy, quiet and hard-working, tall for his age, fair hair and wore glasses.' Despite his excelling in religious studies, he was happy to leave the school in July 1937. After a successful singing audition, he was accepted into the prestigious Westminster Choir School directed by the priests of the Westminster Archdiocese.

At Westminster, Douglas found the atmosphere more

congenial. One of his Westminster class-mates recalls that Douglas

> sang second treble in the Choir and . . . he had a good strong voice. He was a fairly quick boy with a very pleasant manner, brilliant sense of humour and extremely polite. He quite obviously had something 'extra' about him but he was a humble sort of chap and it was never meant to show. He was a classmate and friend to all – even the villains amongst us. With gold-rimmed spectacles and meticulously clean appearance he looked and was a very smart boy.

His father, David, always meticulously groomed, was more than a little annoyed when Douglas, inviting his parents to come to Westminster for an 'Open Day', asked him to come respectably dressed. Presumably Douglas feared his father's sporty, jaunty ensembles would clash with the more sedate attire of the other parents.

His religious bent and poise won him a singular honour at Westminster. He was chosen to serve Mass for Cardinal Hinsley in the private chapel in Archbishop's House on those mornings when the Cardinal was at home. This was a privilege granted to only three or four boys.

He did not fare so well in the sports programme. All his life Douglas was somewhat ungainly and unco-ordinated in sports. He did try running at Westminster and did his best to enjoy the tennis. In fact, he was more at home learning to dance (which he did with considerable skill and grace). He enjoyed the afternoon tea dances wearing his Eton suit with appropriate flair.

On the academic side Douglas was slightly above average at Westminster. He relished singing and his strong treble voice stood out. When he was at the school, the headmaster was Father Launcelot Long, one of the eleven original choristers of the school chosen by Cardinal Vaughan in 1901. Father Long kept brief notes on each boy. He wrote this about Douglas Main just before the Second World War broke out in 1939: 'Pleasing boy – smart – very – mimic – tendency to Benedictines.' In view of what happened twenty years later this was a prescient observation. About a year before, in the spring of 1938, one of Douglas's sisters wrote to her mother, Eileen, from her boarding school in Belgium: 'I got a letter from Doug a few days ago. He asked me to offer my communion .every day for a week so that he may go to St Edmund's [the Westminster Seminary] to study to be a priest.'

What shortened Douglas's stay at Westminster Choir School and postponed further discussion of a vocation to the priesthood was the war. In September 1939, the School was evacuated to the country. Douglas's parents decided to transfer him to the Jesuit school, St Ignatius, where his brother, Ian, was already enrolled. Because of the war, St Ignatius, located at Stamford Hill, Tottenham, was evacuated to a London dormitory suburb, Welwyn Garden City. He entered St Ignatius on 18 September 1939. Because of his years at Westminster Choir School he began in the third form and so was a couple of years older than most of his class-mates. Generally Douglas got on reasonably well though some of the boys considered him a 'sissy'. To his natural poise, Douglas had now added a certain charm of manner. His class-master, chief mentor and, eventually, his close friend at St Ignatius was Father Guy Brinkworth. Father Brinkworth became headmaster of the school shortly after Douglas arrived. He was a tall man with a slightly sallow, rather oriental appearance whom the boys nick-named 'Chang'. It is not clear whether they knew Father Brinkworth's mother was Japanese.

In his first term in the third form, his class-mates elected Douglas class captain. Father Brinkworth's speculation about why they did so is revealing: 'The boys like someone who is a bit above them and apart from them.' Douglas's duties as class captain did not interfere with his work in the classroom. He was good in English and history; not so good in science and mathematics. In his first term he stood seventh out of fourteen and Father Brinkworth, also his class teacher, noted in his report: 'Douglas makes an excellent class captain.' In subsequent terms, Douglas came in the first third of his class and Father Brinkworth's assessments continued positive: 'Douglas has worked well and steadily and is making good progress.' Again, 'I am grateful to him for his efficient work as captain of the class.' Then in the fourth form something went haywire. Father Brinkworth wrote, in capital letters: 'ABSENT FOR EXAMS. A pity Douglas missed the exams. A sound reliable character.'

There were several reasons why Douglas's education with the Jesuits was upset and upsetting. War-time conditions at the school were chaotic – often not enough class-rooms or desks. Classes met wherever they could, whenever they could, in empty sheds, or in a Quaker meeting house. Occasionally, after 'the phony war', the Germans bombed military factories in the Welwyn Garden City area. This turmoil and disorder was bound to affect a boy such as Douglas. Later he would place a special value on order and *inner* stability.

Fortunately for Douglas, the turmoil of his later school days was partially compensated by the Ernaelsteen family with whom he was billeted. Douglas's mother had known and liked them years before in Brussels. Moving in with the Ernaelsteens in September 1939 was a turning point for Douglas. Harry Ernaelsteen (of Belgian and Irish background) was a successful optician in London. He was an elegant, handsome man and a devout Roman Catholic. He was also a man with immense self-confidence who believed you could achieve anything you wanted if you worked hard enough and dressed smartly, and that a sense of commitment and vocation could transform even boring work into an adventure. He often told Douglas he could accomplish great things. In some ways he saw Douglas as the son he never had. The Ernaelsteen family provided a warm focus of order and discipline when Douglas most needed those qualities in the war's early years. Harry and Douglas became close. In October 1941, they were involved in the most serious bombing raid of the war on Welwyn Garden City. Two bombs fell not far from the house and several civilians were killed. Harry Ernaelsteen, taking Douglas with him, went out at dawn to recover the bodies of those killed and to comfort their families. He had and would have a profound effect on Douglas.

Harry Ernaelsteen and his wife, Ivy (with whom Douglas also had an affectionate relationship), had an only child, Diana. When Douglas was first billeted in their home at the age of 13, Diana was four. She and Douglas quickly became pals and played games together. In an interesting reversal of the school play, Douglas was the funny horse, Diana the ringmaster. Sometimes, as part of the game, Douglas carried Diana around standing on his shoulders. If his relatives at Ballinskelligs thought Douglas mischievous, the Ernaelsteens sometimes found him naughty. Once he threw Diana's teddy bear into the fire. Another time he spread Mrs Ernaelsteen's favourite perfume all over the house, explaining he thought it would smell better. But there was always the other side of Douglas, thoughtful and caring. During his first Christmas with the Ernaelsteens, Douglas gave Diana a dog. It was a remarkably ugly dog, but Diana liked it.

However one views his sometimes erratic behaviour (and what was termed 'evacuation trauma' could account for considerable tension during this period), Douglas liked living with the Ernaelsteens. He admired Harry Ernaelsteen's values – generosity toward other people, both in time and money, irrespective of their circumstances or their class. For Harry, people mattered because they were people. Douglas never forgot this. He liked Diana and her mother and he appreciated the regularity that characterized their home, a contrast with the muddle and confusion he sometimes found in his own. So it is not surprising that after spending several Christmas seasons with the Ernaelsteen family, Douglas was confused when his father insisted that he return to London. It was about this time, in early 1942, that the Jesuits decided to move St Ignatius closer to the city. But David's real concern might have been Harry Ernaelsteen's growing influence over his son. When David heard that Harry had urged Douglas to upgrade his wardrobe beginning with several pairs of expensive shoes (later Douglas would always be meticulous about clean shoes), David exploded. He told Douglas to return home and commute to St Ignatius (moved to Hemel Hempstead).

There's no doubt Douglas found this an upsetting experience. It almost certainly accounts for his missing the one set of examinations and it affected his relationship with his father for some time. It did not, however, damage his final term at St Ignatius (which he left in July, 1942). He stood second in a class of eighteen. Father Brinkworth's final report judged,

'Douglas has made really excellent and solid progress.' He was also a member of the Cadet Corps and the Sodality of Our Lady (to whom he had a strong devotion). Some of his peers later joined the Jesuits but Douglas found many of them rigid and remote. He deplored their use of corporal punishment, a practice he eschewed as a schoolmaster himself. Some of Douglas's Jesuit teachers, e.g. Father Paul Kennedy, had their own reservations about Douglas:

> Douglas was a quiet boy, of some ability, very upright. I remember thinking he might easily become a priest. I felt he was slightly immature for his age which I think was about sixteen. When I say immature, I mean too willing to accept, say, what his parents might think good for him or those whose authority he respected, that he had not yet sufficiently a mind of his own. . . . I don't think I was moved by the feeling that he was a possible Jesuit.

Of course Douglas Main did not become a Jesuit. He completed one year in the fifth form at St Ignatius. Rather than remain for a second year in the Fifth, as some others did, Douglas Main, aged sixteen and a half, decided to leave the Jesuits and St Ignatius and try his luck in the market-place.

3

Special Communications Unit No. 4

During his school years Douglas Main did well in English and he liked writing. So it was natural that he should apply for a position on the *Hornsey Journal*, a suburban newspaper, located in the area where the Main family lived in north London. He was accepted and began his journalistic career in July 1942. In his wallet was a journalistic pass number, 23. Unfortunately, his duties were not very significant. The reason was not lack of enthusiasm on his part, but that the war had reduced the paper's impact. For security reasons, the *Hornsey Journal* had no mast-head, and for the same reasons there were no signed stories or by-lines.

Still, Douglas managed to keep busy. As a junior reporter he covered the local courts, council meetings and social events. If the occasion called for it, he was not above a little journalistic licence. Clearly, the wedding of his older sister, Kitty, in August 1942, called for it. Douglas described the wedding lavishly, listed the bridal gifts, then added half as many again for good measure. He was also generous in other ways. With his first week's pay from the *Journal*, Douglas bought his friend, Diana Ernaelsteen, a second-hand bicycle. She describes the scene, 'I could see Douglas wheeling the bicycle up the road. It was in good condition. I was eight years old and Douglas promptly taught me to ride it over the week-end.' Besides the Ernaelsteens, one other stop for Douglas was the local church, St Peter-in-Chains, Stroud Green. Douglas was checking on church news for his paper but he often stayed to chat with the pastor, Canon Aloysius Smith. The parish was staffed by the Canons Regular of the Lateran, a group that would later affect Douglas' longer journey.

31

Besides his work at the *Hornsey Journal*, Douglas was also involved with his family on the war's home front. The danger to their home life at 108 Muswell Hill Road was real enough. All the windows had been blown in by bombs dropping nearby. The church just up the hill had been set on fire by German bombers. Eileen Main was in charge of the red alarm-box located in their home. Their father, David, was a fire warden. Douglas and his sisters were all fire-watchers. During severe raids, Eileen would shepherd everyone onto mattresses under the heavy dining-room table.

Presently the war became more demanding for Douglas. Call-ups were becoming more numerous, so in the spring of 1943 he left the *Hornsey Journal* and took a course as a wireless operator. Then on 13 December 1943, he enlisted at Barnet, Hertfordshire, not far from his home, in the Royal Corps of Signals. He was then nearly 18 years old, and his russet-coloured 'Soldier's Service and Pay Book' described him as 6 feet, 1¾ inches tall, weighing 145 lbs, with blue eyes and light brown hair. He wrote down his trade as a 'student journalist'.

At this time, Douglas's knowledge of the Morse code (some of it learned from his father, David) and the wireless course he had taken gave him a leg up in the Royal Signals. He was sent almost immediately to a training station in Kent. There he spent most of 1944 with his unit (Special Communications Unit Number 3) perfecting the sensitive skills required to recognize and retrieve enemy signals. He was never far from home and his family. That summer David Main had rented a house in Sussex. As the holiday time approached David sent his son a telegram. It read: 'Tell your C.O. to let you home for the week-end for a family gathering or you will be our missing link. Your Daddy.' The sergeant read the telegram to the troops in a booming voice, stressing the words, 'Your Daddy'. Douglas William Victor Main of the Royal Signals was not amused.

In the autumn of 1944 another group (Special Communications Unit Number 4) was formed for more specialized intelligence work overseas. The unit embarked for the European theatre of war in mid-January 1945. S.C.U.4 was a mobile communications unit that included several ambulances containing wireless equipment for both receiving and sending messages. The unit proceeded overseas by landing craft to the port of Ostend. They then moved on to establish a listening base near Brussels.

The intelligence work itself was demanding but not specially dangerous (except for the occasional buzz-bomb). Primarily Douglas and the other 'special enlistment' operators were searching for hostile signals, especially the signals of enemy agents, some of whom were left behind the lines of the rapid Allied advance toward the Rhine. The knack was to pluck the correct signal out of the air, often cluttered with hundreds of signals criss-crossing like tracer bullets. Douglas would sit at a bank of receivers, one to monitor the sender, the other the receptor of enemy signals. (To confuse matters further the signals sometimes emanated from friendly agents).

Of course, there was help to penetrate the confusion. Normally Douglas and his fellow operators would receive a schedule of the special frequencies to monitor on a given day. But if they had no assigned frequencies, they searched for specified enemy signals. This demanded acute attention. Sometimes the listener-operator would recognize the appropriate signal by the manner in which the enemy operator pounded the keys. A secondary task involved locating enemy transmissions by D/F (direction finding). Bearings would be taken on the enemy transmitter from two or more intercept stations. Then the transmitter could often be located, at least in a general area, and its subsequent movements traced. Sometimes the Germans alone had as many as 4,000 messages in the air daily. These were normally transmitted in a variety of codes and ciphers, the most well-known being the complex Enigma, first broken, unknown to the Germans, in 1940. The undeciphered messages, whether from Enigma or other enemy ciphers and codes, usually ended up in a place called Bletchley Park. Located about 50 miles from London, Bletchley Park became the nerve centre for receiving, deciphering, re-encoding and disseminating information from the enemy intelligence system to Allied commanders in every theatre of the war. This information was one of the decisive factors in the eventual victory.

In spite of the pressure of their intelligence work, Douglas and his friends, especially Harry Spendiff and Tudor Jones, had their moments of leisure. Harry Spendiff was an older man. He had enlisted as a policeman from Newcastle-on-Tyne. He liked Douglas and, to some extent, took him under his wing: 'Doug was a hell of a nice fellow, bright, out of the ordinary and definitely officer class.' Douglas also spent a lot of time with Tudor Jones, a shy and retiring soldier from Wales. Jones taught Douglas how to swim and dive and, at Douglas's insistence, they visited almost every church they passed so that Douglas could take a picture. Occasionally they spent a short leave in Brussels or dropped into a bar in Assche for a drink and a visit with a friendly young woman bar-tender. They also got to know and like a hair-dresser of English background in Assche to whom they took cigarettes. Tudor Jones remembers Douglas telling her he would like to become a priest.

Whatever the future held, Douglas did not like army life. He saw the war as something to be endured. He obeyed military discipline because he realized that was the way to endure it with the least inconvenience. He certainly did not relish army food, he did not appreciate the rigmarole of military regulations and he did not like some of his officers (Harry Spendiff characterized one of them as 'a real bastard'). Still, Douglas made some good friends in the army, many of whom he tried to stay in contact with after the war. And he had fun writing poems for his mates. These lines describe the reaction of the unit's brass on hearing Europe had been invaded on D-Day:

> Our Colonel one morning, his headquarters in Bucks,
> Had heard talk of invasion, amphibious ducks,
> His game of golf was near its end,
> Invasion! he thought, 'For my majors I'll send. . . .
> 'Immediate action!' the Colonel decreed,
> Three months later the idea gathered speed.

When Douglas's unit, S.C.U.4, arrived in Belgium on 19 January 1945, the Germans' last major attack, the 'Battle of the Bulge' had failed. Then the massive Allied sweeps across the Rhine into Germany began. After crossing the Rhine in late March, Field Marshal Montgomery (to whose Second

Army S.C.U.4 was attached), proceeded to mop up enemy forces in north-west Germany. The Germans surrendered to Montgomery on 4 May. About the middle of June, Special Communications Unit 4 was ordered to follow the Allied advance into Germany. Henceforth they were based at Bad-Zalsuflen, a spa not far from Montgomery's headquarters between Hanover and Osnabrück. Two months later Douglas managed a short leave to England to celebrate VJ-Day and the wedding of his sister, Yvonne.

When Douglas returned home from Germany to be discharged from the army in the summer of 1946, he had served two years and 285 days in England, Belgium and Germany. He received this testimonial, extant in the Public Records Office:

> Military conduct exemplary. This N.C.O. has been with the unit since enlistment. He has always carried out his duties in a highly intelligent manner and is a popular member of the unit. He is honest and can be trusted in any position.

Until his death Douglas kept a small red address book with the names of most of the men in S.C.U.4. Some of them, such as Harry Spendiff who returned to his police job in Newcastle-on-Tyne and Tudor Jones who went back to Wales to join a small business, he never forgot.

Nor did he ever forget the fascinating intricacies of his work in intelligence. The intense search for the right signal and the appropriate frequency, the discipline required to ignore or discard all irrelevant distractions in the search for the assigned objective, required attention, stillness and concentration. This search demanded patience and, in the face of failure, perseverance. This experience provided Douglas Main with his most striking images for describing the inner search. This is how he drew from his experience in S.C.U.4 to portray an aspect of meditation:

> In a previous incarnation ... I served in the Counter Intelligence Service and one of the jobs that I had to do was to locate radio stations operated by the enemy. And so we would tune in our receivers to them, but the enemy

were very clever and if they were operating that day on a frequency of ninety metres, at eighty-nine metres they would send out a jamming wave, a jamming signal, and at ninety-one they would send out another. So, in order to tune in exactly on their station you had to have an extremely fine tuning on your own radio. But we liked to think that we were just as clever as the enemy and so, when we found out the frequencies that they were broadcasting on, we took quartz crystals and then we would plug in the crystal to our receiver. Our receiver would then pick up their signal absolutely spot on, and none of the jamming devices interfered with it.

He went on to describe how the meditator, like the signaller, required a clear frequency so as to be 'absolutely spot on'. But he was only to realize the full significance of these wartime experiences in another time and another place.

For the rest of the summer of 1946, Douglas, now for all practical purposes discharged from the army, helped his parents move from London to Belfast where David Main had been transferred by Western Union. Then Douglas enjoyed a trip through southern Ireland visiting the family and friends he had missed during the War.

4

The Canons, Dublin and the Law

In some ways Douglas Main's leisurely summer with his family and friends in 1946 was his way of saying good-bye to them. He had decided to test his vocation to the priesthood. In the autumn he planned to join the Canons Regular of the Lateran at their novitiate in Bodmin, Cornwall. It was a curious choice. In England the Canons Regular were neither numerous nor well known. They were called canons originally because they were priests usually inscribed on the canon or roll of a cathedral or collegiate church such as the Lateran Basilica in Rome. Their way of life had been approved by the Lateran Synod in the eleventh century. Thomas à Kempis and Erasmus were Augustinian Canons. Gradually they adopted more of the Rule of St Benedict, expanded their apostolic works and continued to sing the office in choir. This last practice might well have attracted Douglas Main.

Apparently Douglas had decided to join the Canons before he left the army. An entry in his mother's diary (7 March, 1946) refers to Abbot Aloysius Smith who was in charge of the Canons' parish in London (St Peter-in-Chains) near where the Mains lived and which Douglas often visited while working on the *Hornsey Journal*. No doubt he and Father Smith discussed life in the Canons Regular. So, much to the surprise and chagrin of his sisters ('Douglas was always so much fun'), he joined the Canons Regular of the Lateran at Bodmin on 8 November 1946. Some of his former Jesuit teachers, such as Father Paul Kennedy, were not only surprised but disappointed:

I felt the Canons of the Lateran . . . had exerted undue influence on him, that it would have been much better for him to have remained at St Ignatius, where he would have received a better general education, and been more capable of making a real decision on his life.

Douglas's time with the Canons was generally uneventful. His sister, Diane, brought his twenty-first birthday cake to Bodmin on 21 January 1947. She found the surroundings gloomy but Douglas himself in fine fettle. He invited her into the guest room where he proceeded to convulse her by mimicking most of his fellow Canons. After taking his first vows in November 1947, he moved to the Canons' house at Hoddesdon nearby to drive daily to St Edmund's Ware, to study philosophy. His superior at the time wrote: 'He was eminently presentable, popular, of open character and an attractive personality. He always seemed a little uncertain of his vocation as though striving for something more.' The phrase 'striving for something more' was an accurate description of Douglas's motivation for the rest of his life. His superior at Hoddesdon also observed that Douglas was already showing an interest in the eremitical life and he thought he was moving in that direction.

About this time low grades and falling morale were affecting some of the philosophy students. So they moved back to Bodmin and shortly afterward Douglas was chosen to go to Rome for special studies. He arrived in Rome in the autumn of 1949, lived in the College Inter S. Vittore, and studied theology at the Angelicum. But problems began to emerge, the nature of which is not clear. A former superior of Douglas's at Bodmin says Rome was a mistake 'because it unsettles a man of his temperament'. One of his fellow Canons at Rome claims Douglas thought the interpretation of the vow of poverty was too rigid. Another former colleague in the Canons says it was a prank that did him in. According to this version, a group of theology students, including Douglas, decided to have some fun with one of their former superiors, a pompous man then visiting Rome. So they sent him an invitation, supposedly from the British Ambassador, for tea. The pompous superior was elated. But just before he was to leave for the Ambassador's residence, he was told there had

been some mistake. Douglas, so the story goes, was blamed
for the hoax, was dismissed from the Canons and left Rome.

Is there any truth to this story? No one ever heard Douglas
discuss it and some of his former colleagues in the Canons
deny it. What is true is that Douglas left Rome suddenly,
without trying his theological examinations, in June 1950. He
went straight to London to his sister Kitty's flat, took his
religious habit, threw it down the rubbish chute and said,
'Well, that's that!' It was a significant gesture. It certainly
meant Douglas had no regrets about leaving the Canons
Regular even though this represented, in some ways, a failure.
More importantly it involved a maturing process. Douglas
was searching for a spiritual way of freedom, a way that was
liberating. Instead he had found one that was constricting.
Now that he recognized the difference he would be less likely
to confuse the two again. Henceforth Douglas rarely spoke
about his stay of almost four years with the Canons Regular
except to praise them for teaching him how to study.

Douglas Main's ability to study was soon put to the test.
After going to Belfast to help his parents move to Dublin
(where his father decided to live after retiring from Western
Union) Douglas planned to study law. Why would he choose
the law? Harry Ernaelsteen had urged him to do so. Douglas
always respected the rule of law (and its monastic equivalent
in the Rule), but it is unlikely he wanted to practise law. And
he never did so. It is more probable that his choice of law
was another attempt to reconcile his instinct for order with
his desire for freedom. He had been unable to effect this
reconciliation in the religious life. So he would try in the
secular forum. But there was another, more basic motive, for
this change of course. Douglas was already searching for a
level of meaning that went beyond the surface and the verbal.
He wanted to relate to the reality itself, not just to the words
that described it. More precisely, he wanted to relate to words
that described *his* reality, his experience. There must be no
gap between the experience and the words used to describe
it. A verbal, surface experience was not enough. It would lead
nowhere except to more superficiality. Increasingly, Douglas
wanted to authenticate his experience, religious or secular, as

personal. He was not able to do this in the Canons Regular. He would try again in the law.

But first he must get into law school. That was not easy. He applied to Dublin's Roman Catholic institution of higher learning, University College. Ironically the Roman Catholic academics refused to give Douglas credit for the studies he had done in Rome. He then applied to the renowned Trinity College, authorized by the Protestant Queen Elizabeth I in 1592, the university of the Protestant ascendancy, permitting Catholics to enter and accept degrees only in 1793. When Douglas applied in the summer of 1950, the Protestant Registrar gave him generous credit for the work he had done in Rome. Only then did Dublin's crusty Archbishop, John Charles McQuaide (whom Douglas came to respect and like) reluctantly grant the necessary dispensation for him to attend that bastion of Protestantism, Trinity College.

Douglas Main enjoyed his four years at Trinity studying law. He chose courses that were weighted on the academic rather than the professional side. His professors found he had an incisive mind and a succinct style that quickly got to the essential issues. One of his teachers, Professor Frank Dowrick, described Douglas as 'very able, within the top two or three in his class. . . . We had many discussions and arguments about religion and other subjects. It was more an exchange between equals than between pupil and master. He liked arguing and he did it well. I still remember how fond my children were of Douglas.'

Probably no one knew him better than his class-mate and fellow Irishman, Robert Farrell. Douglas was the first person Farrell met at Trinity at the beginning of term in October, 1950: 'I first met Douglas in the University Historical Society – "The Hist" . . . I remember the occasion well – he was sitting reading. There was a large coal fire burning in the fireplace and its light reflected on his glasses. I always thought rimless glasses were a feature of his appearance.' As a class-mate, Robert Farrell was in a good position to assess Douglas's academic ability:

I always thought he was a person of outstanding ability, but not necessarily cut out for law – his interests were far too wide. In a way he was also too capable. . . . How can you be 'too capable'? Well, those who were *less* capable had to work hard and stick to the facts, but Douglas was able to bluff his way through problems that would have sunk other people. He was the sort of student who made the Faculty feel insecure – he realized it himself quite naturally. I remember he said to me one day after he'd been devastating in class on some topic or other: 'You mustn't let your star shine too brightly.' This remark was intended as a note of caution to himself.

Obviously bluffing had its advantages in the academic world. It was even more effective, as Robert Farrell notes, when combined with Douglas's flair for the dramatic:

There were definitely other students who were better scholars of the law, although Douglas would have made a very good trial lawyer. He had a good speaking voice – very astutely modulated. He could be very persuasive on any topic he chose to talk about, and in conversation with Douglas you had to watch yourself that you weren't being fooled. He'd have been devastating with a jury. He had a theatrical side to his personality, useful for a lawyer or a priest. I don't think it detracted from him, but some people distrusted him for it. He sometimes reminded me of Laurence Olivier playing a Professor or a Priest. The only difference was that Douglas did a better job.

How did Douglas get on with others at Trinity? Robert Farrell noted some character traits that caused Douglas difficulty:

He was on good terms with fellow students and Faculty. He was some years older than the rest of us and I think the Faculty found it a relief to deal with someone who was mature and not 'just out of school'.

With many of his fellow students he was rather reserved – I think they probably found him a little distant. 'Reserve' and 'distance' I would say were features of his personality. There was nothing 'common' about Douglas, in any sense of that word. I always thought it created difficulties for him in his dealing with 'the average man in the street'.

Whatever his difficulties in relating to some people (an innate shyness and sense of privacy also contributed to them) Douglas, as Robert Farrell remembers, led an active social life in Dublin:

> His social life revolved around his sister (Yvonne) and her friends. . . . He certainly went to dances, movies and plays. I remember him talking about 'Death of a Salesman' and 'The Playboy of the Western World'. We went to the Sailing Club Ball one year but I can't remember the girl he brought with him. He was human and normal. He frowned on Gung-ho student activities such as excessive drinking. 'Disapproval tinged with amusement' – I would have described his attitude. But he could be very foolish himself on occasion. I remember walking up Grafton Street with him one day. He looked pale and ill and confessed to me he'd been drinking and partying with his relatives from America. 'That was three days ago and I still don't feel well,' he said, shivering and pulling his coat as the wind caught him.

In addition to going to dances, parties, the theatre and being an usher at his sister Diane's wedding, in June 1951, Douglas also found time at Trinity to frequent the racetrack. He followed the horses as much for business as for pleasure. Apparently he had a betting system that worked more often than not. It enabled him to pay part of his tuition fees at Trinity.

Until his final year at Trinity Douglas lived at home where he had set up radios in different rooms to produce a stereo effect. But he had returned home from classes so often to find his mother had shifted all his books and papers (or even his entire room) that he moved into rooms at Trinity for his last term in 1954. In residence he continued a habit that had now become an important practice in his life. He began his day with early morning Mass. Robert Farrell's comment is all the more significant because he was an agnostic:

> He talked a great deal about prayer and the spiritual life. Even when he was a student he thought that prayer and meditation were the answer to the world's problems . . . I

would consider him a religious person, certainly. I don't know how else he could be described. But I'd met religious people before, Protestant and Catholic, and all of them had been bores. It seemed to me that religion had enslaved them – but Douglas was exactly the opposite, it seemed to me that religion had set him free. . . .

This analysis of how religion affected Douglas is remarkably apt. When he entered Trinity College, Douglas was not yet 25 years old. But his attitude to religious faith and the spiritual life had already begun to differ from the views often heard in the Church in which he grew up. Some elements of the Roman Catholic Church in Ireland (and in England too) taught obedience to the letter of the law and warned of retribution from an angry God. This kind of religious bullying too often resulted in a pinched, repressed mode of spirituality motivated by fear. This usually did not lead to growth and freedom in the faith. (Or if it did, it was in spite of the threats, not because of them). More often this approach produced spiritual malnutrition, religious immaturity and the slavery Robert Farrell had encountered in so many 'religious people' whatever their denomination.

Douglas resented bullying wherever he found it, in Highgate Junior School, among some Jesuit teachers, in the secular world or in the religious life. Once, with the insight that sometimes made others uncomfortable, he described a clergyman at Trinity to Robert Farrell as 'a terrible bully'. He rejected any spirituality that contained elements of bullying. For him religious faith should not be constricting but liberating. This liberation was not an end in itself. The end, the ultimate goal, was love. But a liberating tradition provided the inner freedom without which a human being could neither express nor accept love. Any person or any institution that restricted freedom or repressed love was, to the extent that they did so, inhuman and, therefore, suspect. In later years Douglas would develop these themes but they were already present at Trinity. Farrell was right to conclude there was something different about Douglas's religious faith.

There is probably no more dramatic illustration of this 'difference' than Douglas's attitude to the well-known pilgrimage to the island, St Patrick's Purgatory, in Lough Derg in the west of Ireland. In the summer of 1954 he made the pilgrimage with a couple of his friends from Trinity. It is true he tried at the last minute to back out of the project. But finally his friends convinced him to go through with it – reluctantly. The pilgrimage still boasts about its association with 'the Dark Ages'. The pilgrims, fasting from midnight, are rowed about mid-afternoon across rough water to the island, St Patrick's Purgatory, where they remove their shoes, eat one meal a day (consisting of dry bread and/or oatcake and black tea), sleep as little as possible on hard cots, endure temperatures that are usually bitterly cold and 'do the beds', a phrase to describe praying while walking over rocks.

Douglas made the Lough Derg pilgrimage once, and once was enough. As Hugh O'Neill, married to Douglas's sister, Diane, and a Lough Derg veteran himself, said:

> I'm not surprised if he did not repeat it. . . . He considered the Irish to be a nation of extremists. It would follow in his view that when the Irish really wanted to get down to communing with God that they would make the conditions as tough as possible. . . . And I can imagine he would not have found the harsh conditions of Lough Derg to be necessary to be close to God.

This view of Douglas's spirituality is close to the mark. By the end of his studies at Trinity, Douglas had arrived at a spiritual life that required order and discipline, not severity and harshness. Even the order and discipline were not practised for their own sake nor to appease an avenging God. Rather they were the conditions necessary for developing a climate of freedom in which both human and divine love would flourish. These were the themes of Douglas Main's spirituality by the time he successfully completed his legal studies in the summer of 1954. He still lacked a key to integrate these themes. He was to find it in the next stage of his search.

5

Malaya and the Swami

In the spring of 1954, before the end of the Hilary term at Trinity, Douglas Main applied to join the British Colonial Administrative Service (soon to be called Her Majesty's Oversea Civil Service). Like his previous decision to join the Canons Regular, it seemed a curious choice. For one thing Douglas's personal politics did not fit with British imperialism even in its twilight years. His friend, Robert Farrell, observed his anti-imperialism and his growing socialistic tendencies at Trinity: 'We discussed politics a great deal. I would describe Douglas's position as "left-wing independent" in that he seemed to support the socialist viewpoint.' If he were not a conservative in domestic politics, he was certainly not an imperialist in foreign affairs. If anything, his Irish roots and his own intellectual formation as well as his independent temperament smacked more of republicanism than imperialism. So why did he apply for the Colonial Service and why Malaya? The questions puzzled Robert Farrell:

> I'm not sure, knowing his politics, pacifism, dislike of Colonial and Imperial adventures, admiration of Gandhi, it was at first sight a strange choice. But it was an experience, an adventure – Douglas was very curious *about everything* and I think curiosity had a lot to do with it. However, the most likely reason was that it was a job and Douglas was broke.

Whatever his reasons, Douglas received a 'probationary appointment to the Colonial Administrative Service as an Administrative Cadet in Malaya'.

After successfully sitting his final examinations in the Michaelmas Term (his legal degree was conferred *in absentia*

45

in December) Douglas left for England to begin a three-month course of language study in the School of Oriental and African Studies at the University of London. He found lodgings at the British Council hostel for Commonwealth students in Knightsbridge. While there Douglas became friends with a number of the students from Asia. During the autumn of 1954, Diana Ernaelsteen was also in London studying medicine. She and Douglas saw each other occasionally. He invited her to help him choose the tropical gear he would need in Malaya. Later they had dinner at Heathrow airport and Douglas left shortly afterwards to catch his boat for the East.

It was in January 1955 when Douglas sailed for Malaya, a country thought by some to be one of the most beautiful in the world. When he arrived at Port Swettenham on 2 February 1955, the area had been under British influence for nearly 150 years, and under direct British rule since 1874. By the time Douglas first saw the capital, Kuala Lumpur (usually referred to as K.L.), British rule in Malaya was on its last legs. The ultimate cause for their impending withdrawal was the failure of the British to settle Malaya instead of colonizing it. But the immediate occasion for the unravelling of British power in Malaya was a guerilla war mounted by Chinese Malayan communists.

The war broke out in 1948. The Chinese called it 'the War of the Running Dogs', their term for those in Malaya who remained loyal to the British. On the other side, the British called it 'The Emergency' because British insurance companies would honour policies for an 'emergency' but not for a full-scale civil war, which is what the Malayan fighting really amounted to. Thanks to the brilliant leadership, both political and military, of the previous High Commissioner, Sir Gerald Templar (appointed by Winston Churchill at a meeting in Ottawa in January 1952), the Chinese guerillas had virtually lost the war by 1955. Furthermore, the British government had promised Malaya its independence, and a time-table for elections was being worked out.

Although the fighting sometimes crackled in the jungle surrounding Kuala Lumpur, the capital itself escaped the war relatively unscathed. Shortly after his arrival Douglas began his three-year probationary period as an Administrative Cadet. This meant he spent five hours in the morning, beginning about 8 o'clock, studying a Chinese language, in his case the Hokkien dialect. (Later he would have followed some local law courses, because had Douglas remained in Malaya he would probably have been named a magistrate). The milieu of the language school itself could scarcely have been more exotic. It was situated in the ancestral temple of the Chan family, a notable example of a Confucian temple built about the end of the nineteenth century. The temple was still used occasionally as a place of worship and Douglas and his fellow students would sometimes begin their daily studies, eyes itching from the pungent odour of burning incense smoking on the altars across the open courtyard. The British administration had made some arrangement with the Chan family to rent the covered verandas and side rooms that surrounded the main altar. It was all rather ornate with brightly tiled roofs, porcelain fish and dragons decorating the eaves, the home of vast numbers of swallows and bats that swooped in and out during the language classes. After the morning tutorials (the classes contained only half a dozen or so pupils), the afternoons were usually spent studying privately.

Occasionally, as a respite from this rigorous language study schedule, Douglas would be assigned a more congenial task, such as helping to prepare for the first democratic voting (scheduled for July 1955) that would lead eventually to an independent Malaya. It was from these activities there emerged the most famous anecdote of Douglas Main's short tour of duty in Malaya. The electoral officer was explaining voting procedures to a group of natives and Douglas was translating the officer's message. You natives, explained the official, must continue to live by the rules and regulations of the Empire even after the voting. The electoral official waited for Douglas to translate. Douglas then said in the native language: 'We bring you greetings from Her Majesty, the Queen, in London. She has asked me to tell you that if you are ever in London you are all invited to a garden party at Buckingham Palace.' There was a great cheer. The officer

turned to Douglas and said: 'There you are, Main. I told you
if you treated these people firmly, they'd appreciate it.'

Of course, in addition to his other duties and his language
studies, there was a pleasant social side to Douglas's life in
Kuala Lumpur. In 1955, despite some sporadic fighting, the
capital was beginning to relax after more than six years of
tension and fear. As one observer said, in the spring of 1955
it 'felt as if someone had given the whole city a pep pill'.
Undoubtedly Douglas took advantage of some of the pleasures
the capital now had to offer. He lived comfortably enough in
a small bachelors' 'mess'. He and his mates had a servant,
either a Malay or Chinese boy, an *amah* as they were called.
There was also a male cook, and an Indian (Tamil) *kebun*
would have looked after the garden.

When Douglas and his friends ate out they had an interesting cuisine from which to choose because so many of K.L.'s
restaurants, shuttered during 'the Emergency', were now
reopening. The Coliseum was famous for its out-sized curry
puffs served in its mahogany-lined bar and its 'sizzling' steaks
presented on a red-hot iron plate sitting on a wooden tray on
which the steak was cooked in front of the diner draped in a
large bib. The diner often washed down the spicier meals
with *stengahs*, a potent Malayan drink and a favourite of the
planters and other devotees of the Selangor Club, usually
referred to as the 'Spotted Dog' because a formidable late-
Victorian woman once hitched her pet Dalmatian to her
carriage waiting outside.

In some ways the 'Spotted Dog' was the centre of European
social life in K.L., with its cricket, football, tennis and hockey
matches. There were dances and other social affairs. For
the more formal occasions Douglas would wear his white
'sharkskin' evening jacket with black trousers. It is unlikely
he played polo but he certainly frequented the racetrack in
K.L. After a swim at nearby Port Dickson there would often
be a dinner party, perhaps at the Akers-Joneses, good talk,
tasty food and quiet conviviality with friends and colleagues
like Robert Bruce who often shared with Douglas 'long,
delightful sessions over food and drink in which we examined
the problems of the world'. These were the kind of evenings
in K.L. that Douglas relished the most.

There was another side to Malaya that Douglas spoke about little at the time but which he sensed and responded to. It was the side that corresponded to the deep wells of his own Celtic background and also to his continuing search for a spiritual experience that would be real for him. The search for an authentic spirituality, sought with the Canons Regular and at Trinity, continued in Malaya. Douglas's dissatisfaction with his own spiritual life, in a curious way was mirrored by what the writer, Ronald McKie, describes as the 'vague uneasiness' engendered by Malaya which makes

> you feel in this place, among Gods and spirits which have shaped Asia, that at any moment something will happen to you that has never happened before, that you will be influenced by forces over which you have no control. It is a feeling almost indefinable and so illogical that you know it could be true.

Something did happen to Douglas in Malaya that had never happened before and it profoundly influenced the rest of his life. For the first time he encountered an eastern form of spirituality, another way of prayer. More than twenty years later, in his first small book, *Christian Meditation: the Gethsemani Talks*, Douglas Main described this encounter: 'I was first introduced to meditation long before I became a monk, when I was serving in the British Colonial Service in Malaya. My teacher was an Indian swami who had a temple just outside Kuala Lumpur.'

Initially, the teacher was more important than the teaching, for his teacher in Malaya was a remarkable man, Swami Satyananda, a slender, gentle figure clad in a white robe. He was born in the city of Ipoh in the northern federated state of Perak on 15 July 1909. He was 45 years old when Douglas Main, just 29, arrived in Malaya. Both the Swami's parents died when he was a boy of about 10. He was brought up by relatives and educated in a Roman Catholic institution, St Michael's School where, inspired by the teachings of Jesus and several saints, he considered becoming a Christian. In 1926, aged 17, he joined the Malayan Government Service where he remained until 1936. He then resigned to go to India to become a Hindu monk. He spent several years studying

49

philosophy, comparative religions, Sanskrit, the techniques of Yoga and other eastern disciplines. When the Swami returned from India to Malaya in 1940, he became the principal of a school for boys and another for girls. Three years before, when he was 28, the Swami had begun to follow the intense meditation methods of Raja Yoga on a regular basis morning and evening. Later he came under the influence of several holy men including Swami Abhedananda, Sri Ramana Maharshi and Sri Aurobindo.

In 1949 Swami Satyananda founded the 'Pure Life Society'. This was an attempt to translate religious theory into a practical spirituality. It would remain his life's work. As one of the Swami's collaborators put it, '. . . this age lacks God-consciousness . . . the Swami's basic desire was to . . . restore consciousness of the "Kingdom of God" among his fellow men.' To further his purpose of making religion practical the Swami purchased a few acres of land along the edge of the secondary jungle on 6th Mile Puchong Road, just outside Kuala Lumpur. Here he eventually built an orphanage, a school and the Temple of the Universal Spirit on the site's highest point. Adult education classes, a library, a dispensary and a printing press were added later. In 1954 the state government made Swami Satyananda a Justice of the Peace, an unusual honour for a member of a Hindu religious order, almost as unusual as a Benedictine monk being called to the Bar.

Swami Satyananda put great stress on diverse groups living together in harmony in one community. This harmony was realized by the Indian, Malayan and Chinese students who lived in the various institutions of the Pure Life Society. To develop this community life (open to those of any religious background) on a solid basis, the Pure Life Society held regular group meditation classes. Swami Satyananda himself was remarkably practical about meditation. He agrees that images in prayer might be necessary for the beginner, but mental images are only required in the first kindergarten stage. The Swami explains the nature of meditation this way:

Mental worship, together with repetition of the holy name and holy reading is the second stage. Silent contemplation and meditation on God is the third stage. The final stage is becoming one with the Supreme Spirit. . . . This meditation [on Peace] reaches the culmination of our spiritual venture. A serene and silent power is born in the soul of man in the depth of meditation. . . . Let us find this place of Peace – the island of spiritual fortifications *in the cave of our heart*. Let us be filled with the spirit of the Infinite even now.

This was Swami Satyananda: student, civil servant, monk, founder of a community, teacher of meditation, with an honorary law degree, but above all a happy, serene and integrated man. As John Main wrote in *The Gethsemani Talks* many years later:

. . . I was deeply impressed by his peacefulness and calm wisdom. . . . He asked me if I meditated. I told him I tried to and, at his bidding, described briefly what we have come to know as the Ignatian method of meditation. He was silent for a short time and then gently remarked that his own tradition of meditation was quite different. For the swami, the aim of meditation was the coming to awareness of the Spirit of the universe who dwells in our hearts. . . .

Then the Swami elaborated his teaching by reciting several verses from the *Upanishads*: 'He contains all things, all works and desires and all perfumes and tastes. And he enfolds the whole universe and, in silence, is loving to all. This is the Spirit that is in my heart. This is Brahman.' This reading, done with such intensity and devotion, so moved Douglas that he asked the Swami to teach him to meditate his way. The Swami agreed and suggested that he come out to the meditation centre once a week. On his first visit the Swami spoke to Douglas about meditation:

To meditate you must become silent. You must be still. And you must concentrate. In our tradition we know only one way in which you can arrive at that stillness, that concentration. We use a *word* that we call a *mantra*. To meditate, what you must do is to choose this word and then repeat it, faithfully, lovingly and continually. That is all there is to meditation. I really have nothing else to tell you. And now we will meditate.

So once a week for about eighteen months Douglas meditated with the Swami for half an hour. The Swami insisted it was necessary to meditate twice a day, morning and evening:

And during the time of your meditation there must be in your mind, no thoughts, no words, no imaginations. The sole sound will be the sound of your mantra, your word. The mantra is like a harmonic. And as we sound the harmonic within ourselves we begin to build up a resonance. That resonance then leads us forward to our own wholeness. . . . We begin to experience the deep unity we all possess in our own being. And then the harmonic begins to build up a resonance between you and all creatures and all creation and unity between you and your Creator.

This was the teaching, a way to an authentic interior life, to 'the cave of the heart' that Douglas Main had long been seeking, that he first learned from the Swami and incorporated into his own teaching on Christian meditation. In later years Douglas often referred to the Swami, whose death in 1961 at the age of 51, was the result of a car accident. Swami Satyananda's work of making religion practical and open to all still goes on and, indeed, has expanded in Kuala Lumpur through the efforts of his friends and associates in the Pure Life Society. For his part, Douglas Main never forgot the friendship and openness of this remarkable Hindu monk who accepted him as a Christian disciple and taught him to meditate. From this experience there emerged Douglas Main's openness to Eastern religions and to teaching meditation to 'all those who come to pray with us'.

Few, if any, of his colleagues in Malaya knew of his association with the Swami. Meanwhile, he continued his studies in the language school. But he was becoming increasingly disillusioned with the manner of the British transition and the Malayan society he saw emerging. He spoke about this later to his friend, Robert Farrell:

He felt badly about Malaya because he said: 'The British had no constructive policy about anything at all, except to hang onto everything as long as possible.' These were his exact words, as best I can remember them. He wasn't bitter because he was going to lose his job. . . . I think he was just generally annoyed because he felt he was taking part in a sham.

Whatever his feelings about British policies in Malaya, the reason Douglas asked to retire from the Oversea Service (on 30 April 1956), was not because he lacked ability. His superior in Malaya, A. W. D. James, later wrote: 'It was with great regret that I learned of his decision to leave the service. . . . Mr Main had the breadth of mind and depth of insight which are the mark of the best administrator.' And the Director of the Language School, Robert Bruce, described him this way:

He was exceptional. In that large body he had the gentleness of a child. His intelligence was keen, quick and vibrant. He delighted in ideas and readily engaged in argument on the ills of the world. He was not a good student of the Chinese dialect he was assigned to study (Hokkien, I think). I thought he was out of place in the milieu of a brash society – both European and Asian – which was lively but crude compared to the intellectual and spiritual realm which was later to be the home of Douglas Main. He had a good sense of humour and a generous heart.

A part of Douglas Main's 'generous heart' never forgot Malaya, especially the people of Malaya who 'found love in a flower, beauty in a reed'.

6

Dinners in London

After returning by boat from Malaya to Ireland in the summer of 1956, Douglas consulted with some of his former professors and colleagues at Trinity. They needed another lawyer on the staff and Douglas was urged to apply. He did so and won the position in open competition. During the next four years he taught Administrative, Roman and International Law. He especially admired the order, rationality and precision of Roman law. Generally Douglas was popular with both his colleagues and his students. Professor Edward Stuart from the Chemistry Department thought Douglas 'that rare sort of individual with absolute integrity and probity'. A few students found him too cerebral, too Jesuitical and too ready to argue about the number of angels on the head of a pin. As one of his students, Michael Dickson, put it: 'Trinity was neither Catholic nor intellectual – Douglas Main was both.'

Still, students and their professor enjoyed the interesting third-year course in International Law. Douglas was stimulated by the philosophy under-lying International Law, and his class often provoked lively discussions on matters such as the Irish question. Some students remember he claimed it was morally repugnant to support the Fianna Fáil. On this explosive matter Douglas's views were probably more detached and certainly more moderate than many of his extreme countrymen. He himself had served in the British forces, and so had his younger brother Patrick. A fellow student at Trinity, Dermod D. Owen-Flood, frequently discussed politics and the Irish situation with him:

Douglas clearly believed in a United Ireland playing a proper part in the Commonwealth and also in the mainstream of European life. He was not a supporter of De Valera with his cottage isolation politics and, by the same token, he had no time for either the Orangemen or the I.R.A. who were both advocating themselves alone. I am sure he felt the I.R.A. policy of blowing up Ireland cannot bring unity to Ireland.

Some knew him at the Laurentian Society, a social club and meeting place for Catholic students. Mary Lodge, a student, remembers Douglas as

a gently impressive man, very approachable. He was deeply religious and he radiated a quality of goodness. I trusted him. There was peace and tranquillity in him and a sense of presence. I wonder if some of his friends and colleagues really appreciated the subtleties of spirituality evident in him even during the Trinity years. You don't forget a man like Douglas Main.

Thirty years later Mary Lodge Jennings had not forgotten him. Nor had others at Trinity. Dermod D. Owen-Flood remembers:

I would describe him as one of the finest, if not the finest legal mind I have ever met. He had studied Thomistic law in Rome, as I recall. I think this gave him a tremendous edge on his legal studies. He was very definitely cut out for the law. Apart from being academically first class, his ability was leavened with great common sense, fairness and social responsibility. I think, had he stayed in the law, he would have gone to the very top. He would have been a superb barrister and an even better judge. I believe that as a lawyer he would have been able to do a tremendous amount of good for the law and for the community as a whole.

One of Douglas's colleagues on the law faculty, Professor Frank Dowrick, also remembers his flair for the law: 'He could cope with a heavy work load. And that's what we gave him. Had he remained with the law, Douglas would have added to Irish legal scholarship. He would have become a national authority on the laws of Ireland.'

Naturally Douglas Main did more than teach law at Trinity. He lived on the campus in a lovely set of Georgian rooms, where his sister, Yvonne, acted as his hostess for small gatherings, often including students from Malaya. Douglas was on Trinity's wine committee but normally the inimitable 'Slattery' (the college's 'family' butler) would pour the appropriate wines. Later when wine was served Douglas would remark, 'Give it the Slattery twist!' He enjoyed a drink with old friends. Many years later he would write about the pain of 'partings' from friends he loved. On the other hand, he was always happy to meet unexpectedly a companion from the old days. Robert Farrell describes a delightful encounter with Douglas years after they were students together at Trinity:

> Years later when he was a lecturer in Trinity, I met him one day on college green. He had a couple of brown paper parcels under his arm, and motioned me to come up to his chambers. He unwrapped his parcels and displayed a bottle of hock and a record of harp music.
>
> We sat with glasses in hand listening to the music. When the last sad notes had died away we talked about some of the people we'd known and the coincidence of our meeting.
>
> He smiled. 'It was the hand of God', he said, and held out his hand. . . .

Although he enjoyed old friends, good dining, first-class Irish theatre (he once took a group of relatives from England to see *The Playboy of the Western World*), and the occasional dance, Douglas invariably began his day at Trinity by attending morning Mass. He does not seem to have talked much about his experience of meditation in Malaya. But according to his own recollections of this period, he continued to meditate:

> On my return to Europe to teach Law at Trinity College, Dublin, years before the advent of the Beatles and the discovery of T.M., I found no one who really knew about meditation as I now understand it. I first tried to raise the

subject with priest friends but to my surprise my enquiries were mostly received with great suspicion and sometimes even hostility.

As far as I could gather from my conversation these good men practised very faithfully a Jesuit-type of meditation and the best amongst them prepared for their morning mental prayer by systematically going through a list of points for the morning. To me it seemed esoteric and some-what complicated. . . .

But for me personally there was all the joy and excite-ment of the pilgrimage of my morning and evening medi-tation. All the time there was a growing attraction to medi-tation and the morning and evening times became the real axis on which my day was built.

Douglas was also involved in an effort to make the Catholic presence at Trinity more acceptable, especially to the Catholic authorities. Along with others, he helped write and signed a letter to the Catholic *Irish Times* deprecating the ecclesiastical ban on Catholics attending 'the Protestant University of Trinity College'. On another project, the attempt to start a new Roman Catholic newspaper in Dublin, he worked with an influential group of business and literary people including his friend, Garret Fitzgerald – then an economic journalist and later the *Taoiseach* (Prime Minister). Douglas emerged as a leading member of the group. When he realized financial and personality difficulties were too serious, he advised the Archbishop, John Charles McQuaide, to withdraw his support. The Archbishop accepted his advice and the paper never began.

In addition to these activities and his lectures in law, Douglas frequently travelled to London 'to eat his dinners', preparatory to his being called to the Bar at Gray's Inn, a step that would further his academic career at Trinity. While in London he often stayed with his friend and former Trinity class-mate, John Boland, in his Chelsea flat. Boland, who later became the Public Trustee for England, has almost as many stories involving Douglas as there were visits to his flat.

One of these concerned a wedding to which Douglas had been invited. It was a formal morning wedding followed by a reception, champagne and tidbits. For some reason Douglas and one of his aunts missed out on the food. Famished, they repaired to Derry and Thoms, a fashionable store in Kensington High Street. Douglas was wearing a morning suit in full fig, swallow-tailed coat and striped pants. After being seated in the restaurant, they realized they had forgotten a newly purchased book two floors below. Undaunted, Douglas sailed across the restaurant, his swallow-tailed coat billowing behind him. Just as he reached the lift to return, book in hand, a harried looking woman with two children, thinking he was the floor manager, asked, 'Do you sell children's shoes?' To the astonishment of everyone in earshot, Douglas smoothly replied: 'Yes madam, we do. But they're not very good.' As the doors of the lift closed he suggested, 'If I were you I should go elsewhere!'

Naturally, while in London 'to eat his dinners', Douglas saw other friends including Diana Ernaelsteen to whom he had written while in Malaya and from Dublin. By this time, 1957, Diana was 22 (nine years younger than Douglas), had successfully completed several years of her medical studies and was engaged to a young man from Welwyn Garden City, Geoffrey Searle. Still, she and Douglas shared at least two interests, a penchant for long walks (fortunately Diana was tall, almost as tall as Douglas, and lithe) and a desire to make this world a better place in which to live.

So the law professor and the doctor-in-residence would walk half way round London discussing everything from the Roman Catholic Church's teaching on birth control (although she was from a Catholic background, Douglas took a stricter position on contraception than Diana did) to James Joyce and *Ulysses* (Diana thought Graham Greene's *The Power and the Glory* a lot easier to read). One of their frequent conversations was on the nature of socialism: how did socialism relate to a better world? On a walk to Golders Green Hippodrome to see Stravinsky's ballet 'The Firebird', Douglas raised the question of a community of people living together as one possible form of a more loving kind of society. Diana wondered how she would fit into *that* scheme.

In London, in the late April of 1957, the sun was shining brightly and daffodils sprinkled the parks. Douglas had invited Diana to luncheon at the restaurant, L'Écu de France and was waiting for her there with two of his close friends from Malaya, David and Jane Akers-Jones (with whom he had often spoken in Kuala Lumpur about Diana, whom he affectionately called his 'Dutch Vet'). Two Buddhist monks, also friends of Douglas's completed the luncheon party. Diana had to leave early to return to her medical courses. Douglas was a little dismayed. She agreed to meet him the next day.

This luncheon at L'Écu de France began the most intense emotional period in the relationship between Douglas and Diana. They had now known each other since the early days of the war. They met the next day and Douglas remarked casually that one of his friends thought they should marry. Without making any commitment, Diana replied the suggestion was not such a bad idea. During the next few days, while Diana skipped classes, Douglas met her at the hospital and they visited the places they enjoyed, such as the Tate Gallery. They talked about furnishing a home together and Diana pointed to a picture for their dining room. They started walking in the sunshine from Pimlico to King's Cross scarcely noting the distance. Along their route Douglas noticed the little French Church off Leicester Square. He suggested to Diana they go in to give thanks for the happiness they were sharing. They knelt together in the fresh spring light. Suddenly, without any warning, Diana experienced the overwhelming feeling that their relationship was doomed. Perhaps Douglas shared the feeling. Neither spoke of it to the other. They left the soft light of the silent church and hurried down the steps into the bustle and sunshine of Leicester Square. Douglas had to return to his lectures at Trinity, Diana to her medical studies. They parted at King's Cross Station. It was a difficult parting. There was so much left unsaid, so much longing.

For a short time the feelings of 'doom' were suppressed and events moved swiftly. Diana told her parents she was in love with Douglas. She broke her engagement to the young man in Welwyn Garden City. In Dublin, Douglas told his mother, Eileen, then the rest of his family, that he was engaged to Diana and hoped to marry her. Most of Douglas's family did not take the news of his engagement seriously. Most of

Diana's family did. They tried to influence her to break off
with Douglas: he would want a large family like his own
parents; what would that do to her medical career? how would
she manage financially? was she not being unfair to her former
fiancé? Douglas had only loved her for a short time. He would
get over her quickly. He could manage without her. Diana
was susceptible to this family bombardment, especially the
view that Douglas could get on without her: 'this last was
true and I knew it. I believed he could get over it and that
he would find happiness with a nice Catholic girl. I believed
I could get over it too, like the books say. But you don't and
we didn't.'

Meanwhile, in Dublin, Douglas was writing regularly to
Diana. He told her that she would 'adore' Dublin and she
could finish her medical studies there. (Diana was not so
certain. A medical colleague of hers had a difficult time
switching from London to Dublin). Douglas also reiterated
his position that only natural birth control was compatible
with a Catholic marriage. This was a discussion that Diana
and Douglas had gone over many times. It was the traditional
Catholic position on birth control but it was a position that
Diana found increasingly untenable, partly influenced by her
parents, who favoured small families (Diana was an only
child). But quite apart from the moral issue, the practical
problem of starting a medical practice and a family at the
same time was not an easy one to resolve.

It is possible these problems and others, such as the attitude
of both families, could have been worked out, even though
Douglas remained in Dublin and Diana did not even have
his telephone number. He exacerbated the difficulties when
he suggested they write each other less frequently because
their work would suffer. But there was another problem at a
deeper level that Diana had sensed in the French Church off
Leicester Square and that Douglas had wrestled with for a
longer time. How does human love – strong and pure as this
love was – withstand divine love? This was the problem,
grasped by Diana as well as Douglas, that underlay all the
others.

For several weeks Diana (trying to study medicine in
London) and Douglas (attempting to teach law in Dublin)

struggled with an anguish that was splitting their hearts. But the struggle could not last. In the end it was Diana's father, Harry, whom she loved dearly, who urged his 'darling daughter' to make a quick and firm decision about her life:

It seems so strange for all this upset when we should be the happiest of folks, yet I suppose it seems a difficult task for you to choose your life's partner. Unfortunately, Diana, we cannot get everything and no one is perfect.

Your dear Mummy and I only wish you every happiness and whatever your choice we have no say in the matter except if you consult us.

There is nothing against Douglas and although you may have committed yourself one way or the other, for God's sake, darling, make up your mind once and for all.

A few days later Diana wrote to Douglas she had made her decision. She had become re-engaged. Douglas then wrote a note to Diana's mother, Ivy:

I have heard today from Diana that she is re-engaged . . . so I trust that she has now resolved the difficulty in which I placed her.

You and Harry must have been very concerned that Diana had so worrying a decision to make and I must tell you that I am very sorry that I was the occasion of your worry on her behalf. For a few rather delirious days I thought that there was some chance that I might make Diana a good husband. But she has decided otherwise, and I am sure you will understand me when I say that her happiness is my greatest concern.

This note that assumes so much and says so little was like Douglas himself, proper, private, guarded. Except for the words 'a few rather delirious days' of happiness when he thought his future might have been shared with the woman he loved, there is scarcely a hint in this rather formal note of the struggle that had engaged Douglas and Diana too. A few months later Diana was married in the French Church off Leicester Square where she first realized that Douglas belonged to God. In some sense it was her final good-bye.

Both Diana and Douglas had shared the searing experience of a human love subsumed into the divine.

A few months after Diana's marriage, another event occurred that changed the course of Douglas Main's life. His 11-year-old nephew, David, the only son of his widowed sister, Yvonne, died suddenly from an inoperable brain tumour. Douglas was close to David as, indeed, he was to the many children of his own family and their friends. David died on 8 September 1958, the morning he was to start back to school. Douglas went to David's school with his mother Yvonne to explain to David's class-mates that he would not be joining them. Douglas then helped his sister make all the arrangements for David's funeral.

The boy's death affected him profoundly. Later he wrote:

> The death of this child had an enormous effect on me and brought me face to face with the questions of life and death and the whole purpose of existence. As I reviewed my life at this time I was forcibly struck by the fact that the most important thing in my entire existence was my daily meditation. I decided, therefore, to structure my life on my meditation and sought to do so by becoming a monk.

So in the space of a few months, much to the surprise and disappointment of his colleagues in Dublin, Douglas resigned from a promising law career at Trinity College and was accepted, for September 1959, into the Order of St Benedict at Ealing Abbey in London. In one sense the search was over; but the pilgrimage had just begun.

7

Becoming a Monk

Why did Douglas Main decide to become a monk? Why
would a successful academic throw up a legal career that
might have led to the prestigious position of Regius Professor
of Law at Trinity? The question is all the more intriguing
because, in many respects, Douglas Main was a man of the
world. He valued success and had achieved it. He relished
the good things of life, classical music, well-aged wine, the
opera, travel, the theatre, the comfortable service of exclusive
clubs, stimulating companions, vigorous debate, an afternoon
at the races, a night at the ball. With Diana he experienced
the emotion of human love. He thrived in the affection of his
large Irish family who idolized him. At the age of 33 the
world was his oyster. Why then would Douglas Main want
to leave his career, his family and his country to spend the
rest of his life in a monastery in England? Douglas himself
told one of his sisters, 'I don't want to but I must.' He told
another close friend almost the opposite, 'Nobody becomes a
monk because he has to.'

But for him it would not be easy. The sudden death of his
nephew, David, made Douglas aware for the first time that the
inner journey for him would require a parting and detachment
from the good life, from loved ones, from marriage, from
worldly success, a detachment and parting of a kind and
degree he had not anticipated. Much later, when Douglas
Main's closest associate in his final years, Laurence Freeman,
asked him why he became a monk, he said, 'Because I wanted
to be completely free.' This freedom was not a goal, it was a
means to an ever-maturing love. These are the themes –
detachment, parting, freedom, love – that never left him and

they became central to his own continuing journey and to those who shared it with him.

But why England? And why Ealing Abbey? 'Oh, if I entered in Ireland,' replied Douglas with that mischievous twinkle, 'I'd probably give up religion altogether.' And, he explained with another twinkle, a friend had advised him, 'Go to Ealing; they'll take anybody there!' On his visits there Douglas found the Abbey, under its aristocratic and monocled abbot, Rupert Hall, 'a very civilized and relaxed place'. When Douglas arrived in September 1959, the monastery in Ealing, a West London suburb, was thriving. The monks there were running a handsome parish church and a school.

Like all autonomous Benedictine houses, Ealing Abbey follows the Rule of the father of Western monasticism, St Benedict of Nursia (*circa* 480–547). Benedict wrote his Rule (a Prologue and 73 chapters) in the sixth century for the great monastery of Monte Cassino. The spirit of the Benedictines was less regulated than that of the Jesuits, who followed almost a thousand years later, and more gentle than that of the Carthusians and the Cistercians, who broke away from the Benedictine mainstream in the twelfth century.

When Douglas Main entered Ealing to begin his postulancy (about a month) and his novitiate (a year), there was only one other novice, Vincent Cooper. The daily routine usually involved an early rise (5 a.m.), followed by a day of singing the divine office, Mass, personal prayer, manual work (somebody had to clean the 'loos'), study of the Benedictine rule, spiritual reading and recreation. There is some ambiguity in the discussion of Douglas' prayer during this period. His novice master, Father Gilbert Smith was a gentle, simple man, trained in the ways of traditional prayer. Father Smith remembers Douglas speaking about the Malayan swami but not about the prayer phrase or mantra the swami had recommended. Douglas's memory is more definite:

On becoming a monk . . . I was given another method of meditation which I accepted in obedience to my new status as a Benedictine novice. This new method was the so-called 'prayer of acts' – that is, a half-hour spent in acts of adoration, contrition, thanksgiving and supplication, a half hour, that is to say, of prayer that was largely words addressed to God in the heart and thoughts about God in the mind.

Douglas was resigned to giving it a try:

I accepted this development with the same kind of fatalism behind Alexander Pope's: 'Whatever is, is right.' I waited and postponed any serious confrontation with the fact that this new form of prayer was becoming more and more unsatisfactory. And, of course, as I became more and more busy as a monk this fact became less and less urgent.

Meanwhile, he viewed the loss of the mantra as another example of detachment leading to liberation:

In retrospect I regard this period in my life as one of great grace. Unwittingly my novice master had set out to teach me detachment at the very centre of my life. I learned to become detached from the practice that was most sacred to me and on which I was seeking to build my life. . . . The next few years were bleak in terms of spiritual development but I always went back to the obedience which was the foundation of my life as a monk.

His novice master concedes Douglas baffled him: 'I can't say that I understood him. He was different. Sometimes I didn't know where I was with him. I found it much easier to understand his fellow-novice, Vincent Cooper.' But Father Smith was also shrewd. He liked Douglas. He thought him extremely Irish. And, unlike others, he realized how some of the confusion and misunderstandings arose: 'I think he got very close to the Blarney Stone.'

Whatever the different memories about his prayer life, Douglas enjoyed his novitiate at Ealing. He had no regrets about deciding to join the Benedictines. After a few weeks he was clothed by Abbot Rupert Hall at a solemn ceremony in which the candidate discards his lay clothes and is clothed by the abbot in the monastic habit. Douglas liked Rupert Hall, the monocled and archetypal Englishman who had been Abbot for eleven years. They had one argument, naturally about the Irish question. One day at tea the Abbot was flaying the Irish. Whatever his own views, Douglas never tolerated what he perceived as English arrogance toward his own people. He muttered to himself, walked out of the room and slammed the door. Later, having second thoughts, he went to the Abbot's room to apologize. Abbot Hall smiled and said, 'It just proves Brother John, you shouldn't talk politics at tea.' It was at this time also that the new Benedictine novice, christened 'Douglas William Victor' 33 years before, took the name of the beloved disciple, John. From then on he was called 'John' by the Benedictines and by most people. Many of those who had known him earlier, his family and friends, naturally continued to use 'Douglas'.

He looked back on his novitiate year as a joyous one. During the summer holidays of 1960 he went off on a biking trip with his good friend and fellow Celt, Vincent Cooper. Each had been given five pounds to spend. Vincent became increasingly puzzled by his friend's financial manipulations. John did not spend a penny of his own money. Instead, he lived off his friend's allowance. Just as the holiday was ending, John invited Vincent to be his guest in a fancy restaurant where he blew his entire five pounds on a gourmet meal. Then, after ordering a bottle of wine, John, the Benedictine novice, sent it back because it lacked, he told the dumbfounded waiter, the proper chilling.

After his novitiate he was chosen to go to Rome for his theological studies at the international Benedictine College of Sant' Anselmo. He entered the college in November 1962.

John Main found Rome stimulating and exciting. He arrived during preparations for the Second Vatican Council and he experienced the renaissance sweeping Catholic Christianity as the windows began to open. John was exhilarated by much of his Roman experience in terms of its liberation for the Church and for the future. But, much as he relished the bubbling of the cauldrons tended by the church bureaucrats, he always distinguished the non-essential from matters of substance. He recognized that much of the agitation before the Council was peripheral to the essential nature of the changes. These encompassed the waves of hope and the fresh currents of energy that were beginning to reform the Church which John Main had always loved but never feared (then or later) to criticize.

As for his studies, John was a steady average student. Being an older student, he found all the 'cramming' and memorizing difficult (and somewhat useless). He was not a theologian and never would be. He saw no point in carrying around a lot of useless academic baggage. As a result he failed an examination in church history when the examiner asked him the date of a certain church council. John replied he had no idea, then suggested to the examiner he look it up in a book. When he repeated the examination four months later, he passed it easily. The one teacher who seems to have really excited John Main in Rome was Cipriano Vagaggini, who taught sacramental theology. He stimulated John's interest in the relationship between contemplative experience and liturgical prayer. John Main's insight into the in-dwelling of the Holy Spirit, with the implications of that doctrine for the inner life of meditation, grew and matured under Vagaggini.

Of course, away from the lecture halls of Sant' Anselmo, there was plenty of time for fun and games: holidays at a villa near Naples with the American students; hiking trips with the Germans and French in Europe; summer holidays with his family in Ireland. Often John arranged for visitors to be present for the weekly audience of Pope John XXIII at St Peter's. While waiting for the entrance of the Pope, John would point to a vast tomb somewhere nearby and explain it contained a distant relative named Charlie Main. After the audience, the more curious of John's friends went over to peer at the tomb, still clearly inscribed with the name of Charlemagne, the Emperor.

Two sad family events occurred in 1963, Douglas's final year in Rome. In March his youngest brother, Allan Patrick, an outstanding officer with a splendid war record, stationed with the British Army in Australia, was killed in a motor accident in that country. He was only 34 years of age. Douglas, wrote of his shock to his old friend of Trinity days, John Boland:

It has been a great blow to us all. We were very happy in our home life and as well as being brothers and sisters we were all great friends. Do please remember his wife and children in your prayers as they will miss him greatly. Apparently he was involved in a head-on collision in a motor car and so badly injured that he died a few hours after entering hospital. He is buried in Australia at the Military College there where he was acting as an instructor.

The death of his youngest son was especially difficult for David Main. After his retirement from Western Union, David usually spent his spring and autumn holidays at Ballinskelligs in Kerry. He enjoyed chatting and playing cards with his relatives and the 'locals' at the Main's Hotel. Although he had not been feeling well in the autumn of 1963, after Patrick's death he went down to Ballinskelligs in October armed with his regular supply of aspirin and other pills. Usually David's wife, Eileen, did not accompany her husband on his trips to Kerry. She preferred her routine in Dublin. This time she received a telephone message from Ballinskelligs that her husband had suddenly collapsed. Before she or other members of the family arrived, David died, only a short time before his son, John, was to be ordained a priest. John inherited from his father a kind of reckless confidence, a talent for bluffing and a penchant for Irish hyperbole that he never lost.

About two months after his father died, on 20 December 1963, Bishop George Craven, an auxiliary bishop in the Archdiocese of Westminster, ordained John Main to the priesthood in the community church at Ealing. Most of his family and many of his friends were there. Some thought they recognized the little boy in the new priest. In fact, whatever the external perception, John Main had changed through the years. His search for love through freedom, in the Canons Regular, with the Swami in Malaya, with Diana and as a Benedictine monk, had now brought him, through deep changes, to the altar of God. Shortly after his ordination, Father John joined his family in Ireland for the Christmas holiday. The highlight of his Dublin visit came after Father John had gone to Tipperary to say Mass for a friend, an elderly nun. He did not arrive back in Dublin until rather late. But there was another appointment. He and his family waited in the ante-room. At nine o'clock, an attendant appeared: 'The President will see you now.' Father John turned to his mother, Eileen, and said: 'In what other country in the world would the President receive people at nine o'clock at night?' Then they walked into the President's study. Eamon de Valera knelt to receive the first blessing of Dom John Main, Benedictine monk.

After the holidays, early in 1964, Father John began teaching at St Benedict's Middle School at Ealing, where one of his first students was Laurence Freeman. John Main was considered a good teacher although he did not especially like class-room teaching. He disagreed with some of his colleagues about the use of corporal punishment, to which he was opposed. He did not, however, see teaching as a routine job. To the boys (who called him 'D.J.') he transmitted the notion that school and education did not constitute a self-perpetuating, self-justifying establishment but were, in fact, a preparation for something greater. It was the same view he developed of the monastery. It did not exist of, by and for itself. Those who had a vested interest in believing it did, or acted *as if* they believed it, would find John Main both threatening and uncomfortable.

Still, these years teaching at Ealing in the mid-sixties were congenial enough. Father John found time to visit friends including Diana Ernaelsteen Searle who had been nursing her second baby at the time of his ordination. Occasionally he went to the theatre. Sometimes there were no theatre tickets available, and the Main gift for mimicry would then be brought into play. A cultivated parliamentary voice would get onto the ticket office: 'This is the Honourable John Main calling.' Often the tickets would then materialize.

In 1967, an election of a new Abbot at Ealing was approaching. Abbot Rupert Hall's final term was up. Some younger members of the community thought Ealing needed change and more dynamic leadership. They were ready to support Dom John Main, the youngest professed monk in the community. The more conservative group at Ealing rallied round the school's deputy head-master, Francis Rossiter. The third candidate was the headmaster, Bernard Orchard, who had come to Ealing from Downside about twenty years before.

In the event, Francis Rossiter was elected abbot for an eight-year term.

After the election, Dom John was appointed deputy to his friend, Father Bernard Orchard, headmaster of the school. John thought the school's regimen should be modified and liberalized. He could see neither rhyme nor reason to regulations and rules such as school uniforms, that served no purpose the boys themselves could relate to. In matters of this kind he felt frustrated and constricted as deputy-head. But blocked in one avenue, he turned to another. He revived the school's debating society, which did well in competitions sponsored by the *Observer* newspaper. Father John himself enjoyed his morning newspaper. His secretary at the time, Catherine Hay, recalls him reading *The Daily Telegraph* first thing every morning, invariably beginning with the obituaries. She remembers him remarking the deaths of titled friends and his friendship with families of the parish such as the Kruitwagens, members of an international business family, who later helped him in Montreal. Mrs Hay also noticed, as did others, Father John's immaculate grooming. To use his secretary's description, 'He always looked like he had just stepped out of the dry cleaners.'

By 1969 the headmaster, Bernard Orchard, an intelligent and conservative man, had decided, in concert with Father John, that it was necessary for the Ealing school to expand. John Main drew up a memorandum for the Ealing authorities outlining the expansion plans. Father Orchard recalls it as a strong memorandum – perhaps, seen in retrospect, too strong. Nevertheless at the time, Bernard Orchard signed the memorandum as, of course, did John Main. The Ealing community itself was divided about expanding the school at that time. The new Abbot, Francis Rossiter, opted for an indefinite delay. Bernard Orchard felt the expansion plans had already gone so far that his authority as headmaster had been compromized. He submitted his resignation which, somewhat to his surprise, was accepted. Naturally John Main resigned as a matter of principle. Had he not done so it is conceivable he might have become headmaster. The resignations were announced in March 1969, much to the chagrin of the school staff and the consternation of many parents and Ealing boys and alumni. Both Bernard Orchard and John Main remained till the end of the school year in June.

The next period was a kind of exile for John Main. At first it seemed he would go to Australia. Cardinal Gilroy had approved a plan for an English Benedictine to become chaplain at St John's College at the University of Sydney. The authorities in Sydney were anxious that John Main should come. But at the last minute the plan fell through. Instead John Main was sent to Washington to study at the Catholic University of America.

8

Discovery in Washington

Motivated by his sense of obedience but lacking some of his usual enthusiasm for a new project, Father John Main enrolled in the fall term of 1969 in the Department of Religious Studies at the Catholic University of America in Washington. He found his studies, on the whole, lacked stimulus. He had little patience with the elaborate scaffolding of some American academic programmes. Nor could he abide the approach to 'pop theology' that characterized the numerous paperbacks on the subject. However, because of a course in 'Contemporary Issues in Catholic Theology', Father John glimpsed a way of teaching theological truths and especially the workings of divine grace through parables, a method adumbrated in Piet Franzen's book, *The New Life of Grace*. John himself tried communicating divine truth in parable form in an article titled 'A Tale of the Secular City', published in *Review for Religious*, May 1970.

The parable is simple. An old man takes his nephew, a small boy, for a walk through a shining modern city set in a valley surrounded by high mountains. They come upon the ruins of a large building once dominated by a high tower. The boy is puzzled by the ruins. The uncle explains: a group of people built the tower so they could get above the city and see beyond the enclosing mountains. This vision beyond the mountains seemed to give the group of people a new dimension and motivation. They spent most of their time in education, helping the sick and doing charitable works for others in the shining city. Gradually, however, fewer climbed to the top to see the vision. There were discussions about how safe the stairs were. Another faction claimed the foundations could no longer support the structure. Questionnaires were

distributed. A committee was struck to discuss the problem.
The view over the mountains was forgotten. The vision was
lost.

'A Tale of the Secular City' is a kind of allegory or meta-
phor of John Main's own view of life for himself, for the
monastery, for the world. A person must find a way to ascend
above the mundane and the illusory. One must get beyond
one's self and one's environment to glimpse a vision of reality.
This vision can change one's life. But it is a difficult vision
to maintain. It is easier to fall back into the secular mael-
strom, to become involved again with illusion, to lose sight
of the vision in sterile disputes about the means to attain it.
In Washington in 1970, John Main was not yet sure of his
own vision nor certain about the way to communicate it.
During the next 12 years both would become clear.

Often Father John did apostolic work in Washington.
Sometimes he was flabbergasted by the response:

> I had been in America about five months. And I was about
> to give a talk to high school students on religious obedience.
> To my utter amazement, a girl in the front row, vigorously
> chewing gum, stopped long enough when she heard the
> subject, obedience, to say in a nasal New York twang, 'Aw,
> faw-get it, fawthaw.'

On another occasion he was scheduled to say Mass for a
community of religious brothers. He knocked on their door.
A brother appeared and informed Father John straightaway,
'Father, we've written the Mass for tonight.' During the kiss
of peace, instead of saying, 'The Lord be with you,' he was
instructed to say, 'Get switched on, Cat'. The reply was,
'You too, man!' Later Father John would try to find a fresh
vocabulary to communicate spiritual realities to others.

He continued to find his religious studies unsatisfactory.
So in the spring of 1970 he was relieved to be asked, unexpectedly, to become headmaster of St Anselm's Abbey School, a
private Benedictine school for boys situated in the north-east
corner of Washington. The school had been considered a
leading boy's school on the eastern seaboard. Then the headmaster of St Anselm's announced he was leaving his post and
the priesthood to marry a young woman who was also a

member of the teaching staff. Someone, preferably an outsider, was required immediately to get a grip on the turmoil this caused at St Anselm's. John Main, a former deputy-head at Ealing, was at hand. Both the Abbot at St Anselm's, Alban Boultwood, and John's own Abbot at Ealing, Francis Rossiter agreed that John was the man for the job. So, in September 1970, he became headmaster of St Anselm's Abbey School.

The early seventies was a difficult time for most American schools. It was a time of student rebellion, symbolized by the growing drug culture. John Main, ably assisted by his deputy headmaster, Father Michael Hall, gave St Anselm's strong leadership. The two made a good team. John Main, not strong on administration, as the commanding officer, Michael Hall as the chief of staff. Father John (who taught religion in the senior class) reassured the parents of the importance of religious faith. He was also committed to modernizing the school's academic programme. The new science wing was John Main's chief legacy to the school.

John Main's leadership qualities extended to activities outside the school. He initiated a monthly Mothers' prayer group that still meets. With the support of people such as the actress, Helen Hayes, he involved St Anselm's in theatrical programmes at the Catholic University's Hartke Theatre. Among parents he knew well Father John often referred to himself as 'the monk', and not surprisingly he made many friends among the parents and Washington diplomats. They respected his spiritual authority and enjoyed his ironic humour. (He disdained those who thought him a socialite but made no effort to correct their misconception.) Once he described for the Akers-Joneses 'a wonderful weekend at a mountain lodge. . . . The wives brought along a wonderfully civilized cuisine. . .'. Occasionally, Father John would indulge his taste for good music and gourmet food with a trip to New York often with his friends Bonnie and John Hardy, a lawyer on Capitol Hill:

Next weekend I am going to New York for my annual . . . opera pilgrimage to that mecca of music. Opera Friday evening; matinee Saturday afternoon, another opera

Saturday night – all very harmonious and satisfying. I go with two couples who are great friends of mine here. We stay in a lovely apartment.

With some of his Washington friends, such as the Davitts, John Main also indulged his gift for mimicry to set up 'collect calls' from places such as Australia. Jack Davitt had his own theory about John Main's mischievousness and fun:

> On a temporal plane, his 'Irishness' was, to me, the great force that moved him. It accounted for his humour, his ability to spin a tale, to deprecate himself, his love of music, literature and, most of all, of life and people. The current Taoiseach [Prime Minister] of Ireland, Garret Fitzgerald and his wife were . . . his dear and close friends, and on more than one occasion, I recall watching Washington's officialdom, Irish and American, bristle as John drove Fitzgerald to appointments around the Capitol.

Sometimes John told visitors that the large desk in his office had once belonged to the head of the Federal Bureau of Investigation, J. Edgar Hoover. Maybe it did. But John Main's Washington friends knew he was a *schanachie*, an Irish teller of tales. That was one of the things they liked about him.

Naturally not everyone liked John Main. It was inevitable that a personality so strong and charismatic would attract some, repel others. Some envied his life with interesting friends, others were threatened by his successful leadership of the school. These mixed feelings about John Main emerged most strongly in the Benedictine community itself where he had been living. As Father John Farrelly, one of John Main's friends in the community described it, 'John's combination of the freedom of the children of God and Irish spontaneity at times contributed to the problem [of misunderstanding]'. Generally those under John Main on the staff of the school supported him enthusiastically. Others in the monastery were less enthusiastic. Abbot Alban Boultwood felt that John Main unsettled the community while some of the monks thought the community needed to be unsettled. Some opposed to John Main saw him as an opportunist. Others argued he had wit,

75

presence and leadership ability, the very qualities that had revitalized the school and would do the same for the community itself if only he were given the opportunity.

Rumours of the restiveness at St Anselm's reached John Main's abbot, Francis Rossiter in Ealing. If John Main, cosmopolitan, imaginative, sometimes unpredictable made some people nervous, Francis Rossiter, about four years younger, was different. He usually made people comfortable or tried to. Francis Rossiter was born in Ealing, went to the Benedictine school there, joined the Benedictines at Ealing, taught at Ealing and in 1967 was elected Abbot of Ealing. He is a big man physically, good at sports, especially cricket. As a human being, Francis is a pleasant and kindly man. As a leader he is committed to the *status quo* and he does not suffer boat-rockers lightly at Ealing or anywhere else.

So when Abbot Rossiter heard the boat at St Anselm's was rocking, however gently, and that John Main was involved, however indirectly, the Abbot of Ealing was on the alert for trouble. He wrote to Abbot Boultwood and to John himself about the advisability of his returning home as soon as possible. He was worried that John might succeed Abbot Boultwood when the latter decided to resign. (Later Abbot Boultwood changed his mind about resigning.)

No doubt John Main's status in Washington was discussed when he returned home for a visit during the Christmas holiday at the end of 1972. However, the chief reason for his visit was his mother's health. Eileen was not well. She was now 86 years old, and earlier in the autumn she had suffered a diabetic collapse while visiting her eldest daughter, Kitty, on Valentia Island off the coast of Kerry. Father John made a special trip and he and his sister, Yvonne, took their mother to a hospital in Dublin, but her diabetic condition deteriorated. Later Yvonne, with the help of her family, cared for Eileen at their home, where her mother had moments of lucidity.

Then just before Christmas, Eileen fell and broke her hip. Father John came to see her. And, when she died in early February, as he stood beside her coffin he was so moved he could not say the prayers. He had once called his mother 'the gentle persuader'. From Eileen more than anyone else he inherited his gentleness and spiritual depth. She was the instrument of his vocation. He had taken her to dine at his club and had showed her off to his friends. He loved her deeply. There are a few reference points that stand out on John Main's long pilgrimage. His mother, Eileen, was the first. He would miss her.

After his return to St Anselm's from his mother's funeral, both John and Abbot Boultwood waited for Abbot Rossiter to decide about the possibility of his continuing as head-master. The answer from Ealing was 'No!' So, late in 1973, Father John wrote to his friends, the Akers-Joneses, explaining that Abbot Rossiter had recalled him to Ealing at the end of the next academic year (June 1974) and he might come home by Asia if they were still in Hong Kong: 'The only thing is that I detest flying so heartily.' He also explained 'that I shall be glad to get back to the peace and quiet of my cloister at Ealing'. He had begun to find the classroom 'a most stifling milieu' and the political situation upsetting because 'all government now seems to be discredited in the appalling stench of the Watergate mess'.

But it was the 'mess' that John Main discerned in society itself that concerned him most. As he explained to the Akers-Joneses: 'There is a tremendous amount of anxiety about and people live at the very edge of their nervous limit.' Perhaps it was the frenzy he observed during the Washington years that led John Main to question a pattern he saw developing in his own life: 'I often wonder if it is sheer fate or something in me that I never seem to stay any place more than five years. I suppose I should have joined the army and nobody would have noticed it.' There were others who also questioned John Main's stability. The simple answer is that now, for John Main, the place had become less important than the journey. It was not the location that provided stability; it was the steady search. John Main was on a journey to the interior. In Washington he had rediscovered a key element for this interior journey. Now he was impatient to return 'to the peace and quiet of my cloister at Ealing' to test his discovery.

9

London: the First Meditation Centre

Despite his impatience to return to Ealing and his aversion
to flying, Father John chose a meandering route home: a
week in San Francisco, a series of lectures and sight-seeing in
Australia (where he visited his brother Patrick's grave),
hiking in New Zealand and visits to several other cities along
the way. The trip (a gift from the parents of the boys at St
Anselm's) gave Father John the chance to ponder two questions more deeply: were Western monks educating boys for a
life with spiritual values or only for a life of material success?
And what of the role of the monastery itself?

> All through these years in the most success-oriented of all
> cultures I had been thinking of a more really spiritual
> contribution that Western monasticism could make to our
> society. How could we open our own heritage of meditation
> and spiritual discipline to our contemporaries and share it
> with them in the confidence that it was both real and
> present?

Father John told the Akers-Joneses how he was trying to
cope with the frenetic pace of life in the United States:

> For myself I have become very much addicted to prayer
> and devote much time to contemplation. The curious thing
> is that I seem to get more work done and I find that many
> people come to see me – nearly all of them seem to burst
> into tears! Isn't that strange.

What had rekindled Father John's enthusiasm for meditation
was an unusual encounter. A professor in Washington was
seeking help for his son, a troubled young man, who had
experimented with drugs and Eastern mysticism. A friend

78

suggested the professor send his son to St Anselm's. Someone there suggested Father John. Would the young man consult Father John? He agreed. Father John gave him some books on meditation, including *Holy Wisdom*, a classic treatise on prayer by the seventeenth-century contemplative, Augustine Baker:

> I gave him Baker's *Holy Wisdom* as his first book of study, thinking that this would keep him quietly occupied for several weeks, unravelling its loping Drydenesque sentences. To my amazement, however, he reacted with real and immediate enthusiasm, to such a degree that I felt I had to read it again myself. We began to read it together and very soon afterwards we also began to meditate together.

In fact, Bill, the young man, took his daily meditations so seriously he remained at St Anselm's meditating with Father John for about six months. Bill's father often visited St Anselm's during this time:

> From the very beginning I was impressed by the remarkable personality of Father John. He seemed one of the most extraordinary people I had ever met. I went to St Anselm's every few days, as much to meet and to speak a little to Father John as to keep contact with my son. While my conversations with him were always on a rather elevated level, they were not religious nor did they ever deal with meditation at all. . . .

Whatever this experience did for the young man (according to his father it gave him some measure of tranquillity), it deepened John Main's understanding and renewed his commitment to the silent, imageless prayer he had learned from a Hindu swami almost twenty years earlier. The encounter at St Anselm's also moved Father John to ask some basic questions: what was the relationship between what the Swami had said about prayer and the nature of Christian meditation? were they from different traditions? were they related or antithetical? And what about the mantra, the repetition of a prayer phrase? Was this an Eastern, even a pagan practice, or did it also have Christian roots? John Main thought there was the beginning of an answer in Augustine Baker himself: 'In Baker . . . there is an intuitive understanding of the mantra in those passages dealing with "acts" and "those which are commonly called ejaculatory prayers".'

When he returned to Ealing in the late summer of 1974, Father John wanted to research the sources of the mantra in the Christian (and Benedictine) tradition of prayer. In this effort to uncover the mantra, in the Christian context, Augustine Baker led John Main back to the great fourth-century desert monk, John Cassian: 'Baker's frequent reminder of the emphatic insistence St Benedict lays upon Cassian's Conferences sent me to them seriously for the first time.'

So one afternoon in September 1974, with his friend and former fellow-novice, Father Vincent Cooper, he went with mounting excitement to the library in the Ealing monastery. They wanted to refresh their memories on the teaching of John Cassian on prayer. They could find John Cassian in French only. No matter. With growing enlightenment they read chapter 10, entitled, 'The Second Conference of Abbot Isaac on Prayer'. The story told there is a simple one. Two young friends, Cassian and Germanus, fed up with their attempts at prayer, want to learn to pray more effectively. They visit monasteries and consult gurus without satisfaction. Finally they travel to the Egyptian desert (as thousands of young Westerners have travelled to the East seeking enlightenment today). In the desert they visit Abbot Isaac, a master of prayer. He spoke to them of the beauty and efficacy of continual prayer. Cassian and Germanus left for home bubbling with enthusiasm. Then they realized, although Abbot Isaac had extolled continual prayer, he had not said a word about *how* to pray.

Cassian and Germanus returned to Abbot Isaac. They asked him, 'how we can arrive at that condition in prayer, of which you discoursed. . . .' Lacking what they called 'some simple rudiments' to pray, they told Abbot Isaac they were more bewildered then ever by the gap between their conviction about prayer and their experience of it. How many modern people have experienced the same difficulty, their desire to pray frustrated by modalities of prayer that so often led in circles not to God but back to self?

Abbot Isaac told them their desire to pray already placed them on the path of prayer. He answered the question, 'How do I pray?' by referring to the experience of the old man called Serapion. For forty years, Serapion, an elder in the desert, had prayed to a god with a human bodily structure. Serapion and the other Anthropomorphites 'supposed that God possesses eyes, a face, and hands and other members of a bodily organization'. This aberration arose from taking too literally those passages in Scripture in which God is spoken of, analogously, in human terms. The result of this kind of 'image' prayer is not only unsatisfactory to the person praying; it reduces God to human terms, it trivializes him.

Having placed the problem of prayer in its broader context – making a human image of God will not make God or prayer more real, just more illusory – Abbot Isaac then gives Cassian and his friend, Germanus, a 'formula' for prayer 'which every monk in his progress towards a continual recollection of God is accustomed to ponder, ceaselessly revolving it in his heart, having got rid of all kinds of other thoughts'. This prayer formula, from the Psalms, comprises the familiar phrase, 'O God, make speed to save me: O Lord, make haste to help me', the words used by St Benedict at the beginning of the Divine Office. Cassian recommends this 'saving formula' for all as an antidote to 'interruption and images of vain figures and the recollection of conversations and actions', an apt description for distractions. Cassian insists he is talking about 'imageless prayer'. The meditator 'is not merely not engaged in gazing on any image, but [this prayer] is actually distinguished by the use of no words or utterances'.

Then in one of his richest concepts, Cassian speaks, para-doxically, about those with enough detachment to meditate on this single verse becoming 'grandly poor' in the spirit of the beatitudes:

This is the formula which the mind should unceasingly cling to until, strengthened by the constant use of it and by continual meditation,. it casts off and rejects the rich and full material of all manner of thoughts and restricts itself to the poverty of this one verse.

So the hour spent in the library at Ealing in the late summer of 1974 studying a man who had lived in the Egyptian desert 1,600 years before, paid rich spiritual dividends. It had confirmed John Main's intuitive discovery that the simple practice of a prayer formula or mantra, first learned from a Hindu swami, had Benedictine and Christian roots going back through Augustine Baker to John Cassian in the fourth century and beyond.

Exhilarated by his rediscovery of a Christian prayer from the East that had been virtually lost to the West, John Main was now able to reconcile his experience of Eastern meditation with his own Benedictine tradition. This was a profound and exciting insight and one that would have far-reaching consequences. These began almost immediately at Ealing. Father John received permission from Abbot Rossiter to establish a small lay community at Ealing primarily devoted to the practice of meditation. As John Main explained: 'The tradition out of which we would teach was that of Western monasticism from its beginning: the teaching of John Cassian invoked as a spiritual guide in the Rule, and St Benedict's "teacher of prayer".' In establishing his first house for meditators, John Main paid special attention to younger people. What are we doing, he would ask, for the spiritual life of our youth? A lay community at Ealing in a large house, a former novitiate, was the first step. About the same time The Grail (a secular institute) sponsored the first meditation group a few miles away at Pinner.

By the beginning of 1975, the new lay community house was ready to receive its first applicants. Four young men came to live and to learn to meditate. They included Laurence Freeman, who later would become Father John's closest associate in the work of teaching Christian meditation. Laurence Freeman was born in Kensington, London, in 1951, his father a chartered accountant, his mother a nurse. Shortly after he was born his parents separated, the children, Laurence and twins ten years older, remaining with their mother. Laurence began school at the Ealing monastery in 1958, about a year before John Main joined the Benedictines. He graduated from Ealing in 1969 and began working, eventually full-time, in the youth section of the United Nations. Later the same year, Laurence, a slim, intense, somewhat shy and extremely bright young man of 18 went to New York, where he became a general assistant to the British Ambassador to the United Nations, Lord Caradon.

Occasionally, while in New York, Laurence travelled to Washington to see his former teacher and mentor, Dom John Main. In the autumn of 1970, Laurence went up to Oxford to study English, which he did successfully for the next three years. At Easter 1972 he visited Washington again, and this time Father John introduced him to Christian meditation. In 1973 he decided to take a year off from university. Always interested in writing and journalism, Laurence wrote free-lance articles for publications such as the BBC's *Listener* magazine. To supplement his income Laurence joined a merchant bank. Two years after leaving Oxford he decided he would not go back. He had a visit with Father John after the latter's return from Washington in the late summer of 1974: 'I told Father John I'd been thinking about becoming a Jesuit. He dismissed the idea out of hand. It was, of course, his way of testing it. Anyway, I decided to try the lay community for six months.'

Later, in the spring of 1975, in addition to Laurence Freeman and the three other young men who joined the new lay community, people came from Ealing parish and elsewhere, among them Lady Lovat, wife of the renowned Lord Lovat, a commando chief during the war. Lady Lovat had previously made a retreat under Father John. She and the others came to inquire about learning to meditate with the rapidly forming prayer groups. These (coming to the meditation centre weekly) soon numbered nine.

Father John was 'clear that the essential way to teach others how to pray was to pray with them'. From this experience of praying together '. . . we gradually developed, in our opening talks, a theology of meditation based on the "secret" of St Paul's letters, the indwelling secret of Christ in you!' For a long time Father John had struggled to relate what he had learned from the swami about *how* to pray, about silence and the interior journey, with what he later came to understand about the riches of Christian theology:

... it was not until ... years later after I learned to meditate with him [the Swami] that I began dimly to understand what my master had taught me and to understand the incredible richness of its full exposure in the Christian vision. This was when I studied the doctrine of the indwelling of the Holy Spirit with Dom Cipriano Vagaggini in Rome.

Father John's realization of the Pauline 'secret', the real presence of the risen Christ in the human heart, had been articulated by writers such as the Dominican, Yves Congar in *The Mystery of the Temple* and the Jesuit, Père Jean-Pierre de Caussade in *The Sacrament of the Present Moment*. It was rooted in the teaching of Cassian, Benedict and Augustine Baker. This meant Father John's understanding of prayer was simple, basic and deeply grounded in Scripture and tradition. Is there, however, a problem inherent in this way of prayer? On the one hand the Scriptures praise unceasing prayer; on the other the Scriptures say creatures do not know how to pray. For Father John there was no problem because there was only one prayer. This was the prayer continually ascending from the risen Jesus (indwelling in the human heart) to the Father. Our prayer is not to concoct some prayer of our own. Our prayer is to become present through silence and, in faith, to the prayer of Jesus rising from 'the cave of the heart' to the Father:

> We have to realize that when we talk about 'our prayer' we are really talking about disposing ourselves for the full liberation of the life of the Spirit within us, which is the prayer of Jesus and his vital connection with the Father. This is why we pray to the degree that we turn away from ourselves, from the possessive self-consciousness and trivial distractedness of everything we sum up as ego. . . .

In Father John's view, the greatest enemy of simple prayer, as a participation in Christ's experience with the Father, is the human imagination:

> I do believe, and believe it is the belief of the tradition (experience and tradition being one again) that the more we 'think' about God, picture him, or stir up our imagin-

ation for autonomous visions of him, the less we can experience him. This is not to denigrate theology, philosophy or art. But these three fruits of our minds and hearts have value for ultimate meaning only so far as they clarify, encourage, or purify our journey to the frontiers of the limited human consciousness. On this frontier we are met by a guide, who is unlimited consciousness, the Person of Jesus Christ.

But how does a person dispose himself or herself to participate, in faith, in the prayer of the risen Jesus to the Father by turning away from the imagination and from the ego? It is here that Dom John Main makes a basic contribution to the spiritual life by his rediscovery of the mantra. Through the continual silent repetition of a prayer phrase or mantra, the meditator turns away from the imagination and self-consciousness toward an interior silence where God is discovered not in the illusion of imagery but in the reality of faith:

> . . . all Christian prayer is a growing awareness of God in Jesus. . . . And for that growing awareness we need to come to a state of undistraction, to a state of attention and concentration – that is to a state of awareness . . . the only way that I have been able to find to come to that quiet, to that undistractedness, to that concentration, is the way of the mantra.

The mantra that John Main himself recommended was the Aramaic phrase, 'Maranatha' (Come, Lord Jesus): 'I recommend it because it is in Aramaic, the language Jesus himself spoke, because it's probably the most ancient prayer in the Church: St Paul ends Corinthians with it, John ends Revelation with it, it can be found in the Didache. . . .'

In dealing with the significance of the mantra, John Main remains consistent in his view that the way of prayer is not a way of images, thoughts, memories and ideas, thereby reducing God to human dimensions. All this mental baggage must be cast off and set aside. So, says John Main, must the meaning of the mantra itself. In this he goes beyond Cassian and is closer to the writer of *The Cloud of Unknowing*:

Throughout the *Cloud of Unknowing* the author urges us to choose a word that is full of meaning; but that once you have chosen it, to turn from the meaning and associations and to listen to it as sound. 'Maranatha' is a perfect mantra from that point of view.

So the meditator not only gives up in prayer all the fruits of his intellect and imagination, the meditator also casts off the meaning of the mantra. Saying the mantra continually is the first step on the interior journey to participate, in faith, in the prayer of Jesus to his Father. Using a human idea, a human image, even the meaning of a human mantra would only stall the journey at the human level. Still, the mantra must be said, silently, soundlessly, interiorly, continually for the full time of the meditation (about a half hour). John Main, however, never gave hard and fast rules about the manner of saying it:

> Most people say it in rhythm with their breathing. The important thing is to articulate it clearly in the silence of your mind, a silence that is itself deepening and spreading all the time, and to concentrate on it to the exclusion of all other thoughts . . . you begin by saying it, you then sound it in your heart and finally you come to listen to it with total attention.

John Main made no effort to force the mantra and Christian meditation on anyone. If people displayed lack of interest or hostility, Father John did not argue with them. (He had an instinctive sense about those who would be interested in Christian meditation and those who would not; he would not even raise the subject with the latter group, among whom were some of his friends.) But if anyone showed interest, John Main took the time to share his own experience of prayer, as in this letter to a nun who had inquired about the mantra:

> Saying the mantra is as easy as falling off a wall: all you do is to begin to say it in your mind – then sound it – next is listen to the sound of it. The only quality you then require is simplicity – to keep saying it. 'Unless you become as little children.' What word does a child keep repeating: 'Abba, Father'. Each repetition is a new confidence estab-

lished – not because the child *thinks* about it, but because the child experiences the relationship as *real*. That is what the mantra is about – no thought, no imagination: only PRESENCE.·

This was John Main's simple teaching at the meditation centre at Ealing. The prayer meetings began with some appropriate music, and then the group listened to a brief instruction from Father John that amounted to: 'Sit down, sit erect and say your mantra.'

Father John was also teaching Christian meditation to other groups. Not long before he finally left Ealing, he gave a thirty-day retreat to the Medical Missionaries of Mary (an Irish Congregation with missions in Africa and elsewhere) at a convent in Wimbledon in London. It was during this retreat that Father John stressed the dynamic and contemporaneous nature of Christian meditation. He contrasted it with the 'unspiritual religiosity' of those who opt to live in the past, and with the 'cultivated anticipation' of those who prefer to live in the future.

In terms of prayer, the first group finds it easier to return to the life of the historical Jesus. The danger of this historical reverie is that people lose contact with the risen Jesus present and alive, in the human heart. This first group refuses to enter completely into the present moment and so, in a spiritual sense, never become men and women 'fully alive'.

The other group opts for a 'cultivated anticipation' of the future. These people are busy about many things – their work, their spiritual reading, their friends, their apostolate. This group says: 'One day I'll have time to live in the presence of God. Now I must get on with my work.' Both groups have this in common. They miss the reality of the present moment, the 'now' that St Paul called the acceptable time. As John Main put it at the Wimbledon retreat: 'We can't live on past religious capital or on future religious development. . . . In meditation we seek to enter fully into the "now" with the Lord Jesus risen and alive in our hearts.'

John Main, of course, was clear about the importance of the historical Jesus. He simply claimed the essential message of the New Testament is that 'the Lord Jesus lives in my heart' and the historical life of Jesus must be seen from and through *that* perspective. The primary concern of Christian meditation is with neither the future nor the past. It is to respond wholly to the here and now, to be men and women 'fully alive' to the reality of the present moment.

One of the Medical Missionaries who made Father John's Wimbledon retreat, Sister Miriam Quigley, remembers how profoundly she was affected:

He gave me a whole new understanding of the Scriptures because he gave us an entirely fresh appreciation of prayer. Prayer is not talking to God *but being with him*. Prayer is an awareness of being loved. Prayer is that stream of love between the spirit of the risen Jesus and his Father in which we are present. We must make our presence real, in faith, by repeating our little word, our mantra.

On one occasion during the retreat, Sister Quigley went to Father John's room and asked if she might pray with him. They prayed together in silence for about fifteen minutes: 'His presence alone geared you to prayer. When one was in Father John's presence one was filled with joy. You felt he loved you. And he led you to the Father.'

By now Father John had become a superb teacher, mainly because in his later years at Ealing he had deepened and clarified what he wanted to say. These were not altogether easy years. Once John Main wrote to Sister Miriam Quigley (who had also found her stay in her Ealing convent a difficult experience), 'I saw you in a backwater like Ealing where we were both marking time and God was marking us.'

In less than ten years John Main was marked and shaped by three experiences. First, by his exile from Ealing over the issue of school expansion; that was a humbling experience. He was marked in another way by rediscovering meditation in Washington and deepening that discovery at Ealing; those were enlightening experiences. Thirdly there was John Main's involvement in elections for Abbot both at St Anselm's and at Ealing; these were painful experiences. All these events had one thing in common. For John Main, ultimately, they were profoundly liberating. But there was still the time of marking at Ealing.

Since his return from Washington in the autumn of 1974, John Main, despite the development of the meditation centre, was in a sense marking time in the Ealing community. His friend and former headmaster, Father Bernard Orchard, thought Abbot Rossiter should have appointed John to head the school which was faltering. But the Abbot declined, apparently because he judged John Main's leadership too unpredictable. Instead Abbot Rossiter made him the head librarian, a routine assignment that John turned into a challenge by refurbishing Ealing's library from top to bottom.

This reaction was typical. John Main had the ability to transform a humdrum task or a potential disaster into an adventure. Once, shortly after returning from Malaya, he was staying with friends in Chelsea. He had a gift from Malaya, a bright flower-decked silk dressing gown and a pair of matching silk slippers that turned up at the toes. Early one morning, dressed in this oriental garb, he went downstairs to fetch the milk from the front door. Just as he bent over to pick up the bottles, he slipped on the icy street. He landed on his back beside the porch steps and near a queue waiting for a bus, firmly holding up a bottle of milk in each hand. A young girl, of about ten, looked down astonished at this tall man swathed in oriental silks holding up two milk bottles. 'What on earth are you doing?' she inquired. In a grave tone, John Main replied, 'I do this every morning before breakfast.'

Whatever John Main's capacity to find excitement in the routine, his work in the library was ending. So was Francis Rossiter's first term as abbot. Even before he returned from Washington, a group of Ealing monks, especially younger ones, urged John to be a candidate. He did not need much urging. John Main was a confident man, some would say overly confident. He had strong views on the nature of monasticism and the adaptations required by monastic communities to make them relevant in the twentieth century. These views appealed to many of the younger monks at Ealing. He summarized these ideas in a talk he gave to the Ealing community after the election. The work of the monastery, he told his brother Benedictines, must be defined by its prayer life, not the other way round. The Rule is not so much the guardian of the *status quo* as a compendium of values for

89

monks who have begun the pilgrimage. St Benedict's approach to monasticism was dynamic, not static. There is a constant danger the works of the monastery will become an escape from prayer, not its natural fruit.

What about the role of the abbot? John Main did not see the abbot as primarily an administrator or permission-giver but as in St Benedict's vision, where the abbot is much more a charismatic figure. His charism is for teaching, inspiring and encouraging all those who have seriously embarked on the monastic adventure. Part of the abbot's charism will create a climate and a style of life that is conducive to *real community* where there is the opportunity for genuine communication and affection among the members. The abbot must ensure that the result of obedience to the Rule is a fully human life where 'the whole man, body and soul is making the pilgrimage, no one reaching the goal of holiness without having achieved his own wholeness'. Then John Main, in his talk to his brother monks at Ealing, returned to the order of priorities that would continue to guide his own monastic vision. No religious community, he felt, is justified merely by what it does but by what it is. The community must find a way of prayer that transforms it at the centre. It must be christocentric and its apostolic works must emerge from this centre to which it must constantly return in prayer.

This was an energizing view of the contemporary monastery, requiring radical change, and it had a powerful influence on many of the monks at Ealing. Like most religious communities of its time Ealing Abbey experienced the tension between conservative and progressive views. In a simplified way, the Ealing monks broke down into two categories: those who wanted change and those who were satisfied with the *status quo*. Those who sought change also comprised two groups: those who wanted modifications in the monastery's apostolic works, such as the parish, and the school; and the others who wanted fundamental renewal and reform in the life of the monastic community itself. It was from among this last group that John Main's strongest support came.

There is no doubt that John Main wanted to be Abbot of Ealing. He felt he could bring a new vision to the monastery and could do more to attract young men to become monks

London: the First Meditation Centre

of Ealing. Many, though not all, of the younger monks shared
Father John's vision, and of those who did, not all shared his
total vision. Some of Father John's friends had changed their
views during the years he was away in Washington. As his
friend, and former teaching colleague, Father Anthony Gee
explained it: 'John was like a big tree and when he was
there the smaller trees couldn't grow. When he was away in
Washington the smaller trees grew. When he came back the
younger Ealing-ites were more independent.' This meant that
some of the younger monks would support John but only so
far. Others questioned his motives and steadiness. Was he
too ambitious? too visionary? Where would he take Ealing if
he were to become abbot? Before the election there was a
rumour floating about that John Main, if elected, would get
rid of Ealing's television sets.

Where John Main would have taken Ealing (with or
without television sets) is a moot point. In an extremely
close abbatial election in July 1975, John Main fell short of
becoming abbot, some say by one vote. The former abbot,
Francis Rossiter, was re-elected for a second term of eight
years. The results were a relief to those who liked Ealing the
way it was; a disappointment to those who shared John
Main's vision of a more contemporary monasticism. There is
no doubt John Main was disappointed and frustrated by the
outcome.

His disappointment was heightened by an almost identical
result in a similar election a few weeks later. After twenty-
seven years as Abbot of St Anselm's in Washington, Alban
Boultwood resigned in September 1975, and elections for a
successor were held the same month. In some ways the
abbatial election in Washington was a re-run of the one in
Ealing. Many of the younger monks, especially those associated with Father John in the school, remembered his vigorous
and successful leadership as headmaster and favoured him
to succeed Abbot Boultwood. The outgoing abbot himself
summarized the fears of those who opposed John Main:

John Main was ambitious to be Abbot. He would, if he
were elected, stress the social side of the Abbot's office.
[Some of the monks at St Anselm's resented John Main's

social and diplomatic friends]. He had disturbed the community. Why should we revive all the disturbance by electing him Abbot? Could he take the rough decisions that an Abbot must take? Would he be prudent?

These questions, like the ones at Ealing, remain moot. Although he had been absent from Washington for more than a year, John Main received strong support from those who knew him best and had worked with him as headmaster. But again he lost the election by a narrow margin.

What effect did this rejection, coming so quickly after the one at Ealing, have on John Main? To say that he was shattered is to over-state the case. To say that he was relieved not to have the responsibility is to under-state it. It is the long-term significance of the set-back that is important. Ironically, the loss of the abbatial elections eventually provided John Main with the external liberty and the internal detachment so necessary to pursue his inner journey. John Main's response to failure was not bitterness. It was, ultimately, a radically new direction.

After losing the abbatial election at Ealing, John Main was appointed prior of the monastery and novice master. Although these were positions of trust neither totally absorbed his energies. The prior in a Benedictine monastery, in theory the number-two man under the Abbot, is in practice often a supernumerary. He was such under Abbot Rossiter who, like many religious superiors, did most things himself. There was only one novice at the time, Laurence Freeman, who at the end of 1975, decided to join the Benedictines at Ealing.

Because his talents were under-utilized in the community, Father John spent more time away from Ealing giving retreats and conferences in Ireland, America and in England, always stressing Christian meditation. He used every medium as he told the Akers-Joneses: 'Recently I entered the mad world of commercial broadcasting, in a "phone-in" programme on meditation! Quite a strange experience but not without its funny side.' (Some years later Father John participated in a similar programme, hosted by myself, in Montreal.) In the spring of 1976 Father John was chosen by Abbot Basil Hume, soon to be Cardinal Archbishop of Westminster, to give the

prestigious retreat at the Benedictine monastery of Ampleforth. Father John wrote about preparing for the retreat with
his customary wit to his former deputy at St Anselm's, Father
Michael Hall: 'I am putting my final touches to my talks for
the Ampleforth retreat – Poverty with three million in the
bank. Problems on chastity on a windswept Yorkshire moor.
How to be obedient when your former Abbot becomes Pope,
etc., etc.'

Much as he was energized by these apostolic activities,
John Main was becoming increasingly discouraged by the
situation at Ealing. He thought the work of the monastery was
less and less relevant to the needs of contemporary people,
especially younger people. Often he shared his misgivings
with Father Michael Hall. Father Michael, then 37 years of
age, was thirteen years younger than Father John. He had
always lived in Washington where his father had worked in
the health offices of the federal government. Michael Hall
was educated by the Benedictines at the priory school from
which he graduated in 1956. After studies at Georgetown
University in Washington he joined the Benedictines in the
summer of 1958, a little more than a year before John entered
the novitiate at Ealing. Michael was ordained to the priesthood in February 1965. Later he studied at the Catholic
University of America, at Cambridge and at McGill University in Montreal. He first began teaching at St Anselm's in
1961 and was appointed assistant headmaster in 1968. When
Father John became headmaster in the autumn of 1970 Father
Michael remained as his deputy. Both monks shared an
interest in the future of monasticism. By the end of John
Main's headmastership at St Anselm's, Michael Hall believed
John wanted to be the leader of a group of religious men in
a small monastic community that revolved on prayer.

10

Goodbye to Ealing

At the beginning of August 1976, John Main's musings about a new foundation were beginning to clarify. One reason, as he explained to Michael, was the deteriorating community situation at Ealing: 'We are drifting without a policy, without any real unity – just getting the day-to-day chores done.' John Main had reached a turning point:

> I have now come to the firm conclusion that we simply must make a foundation. Before we are all too old in this one life we have to lead we must make the courageous step . . . we have really to try to achieve the monastic vision in a new way.

Then John Main got down to brass tacks. Would Michael Hall let him know about the possibilities for a new foundation in the United States? He had been thinking of three alternatives to Ealing: taking over a city church in London, such as St Bride in Fleet Street, and running it as an ecumenical centre with the Anglicans, stressing meditation; reviving a collapsing monastery in Europe; or starting with a parish attached to a German or Austrian monastery. But who would join such an enterprise? John felt two or three from the Ealing community, some of the new lay community, and several nuns who had expressed interest: 'We must see to it that we do not just keep this at the level of talking but do actually get moving.' Finally, in this letter to Michael Hall, Dom John notes he has discussed most of these alternatives with his abbot, Francis Rossiter.

During the summer of 1976, John Main's search for alternatives was both extensive and somewhat indefinite. But one theme remains constant: there must be a facility for instruction in prayer and for praying together. About this time (the middle of August 1976), a visit from a couple in Montreal might well have had some indirect influence on John Main's initial interest in Montreal. Hans and Margaret Kruitwagen, friends of John Main's when they lived in Ealing were now living in Montreal. They lunched with John in London that August and told him how much they liked Canada and Montreal. They also invited him to visit them there.

Soon afterwards Father John mentioned the possibility of Montreal to Eileen Byrne, a Sister of Sion living outside her community in Ealing. She had joined the first meditation group there in 1974 and she had spent several months in the Montreal area and knew some of the people in the Chancery Office there. So it was natural for Father John to tell her he might be going to Montreal and to ask her to try to arrange a meeting with the Bishop in charge of English affairs in that bilingual city, Bishop Leonard Crowley. Eileen Byrne wrote to a friend, Father Bob Harris, on the Bishop's staff, asking to arrange a meeting.

While waiting for an answer Father John continued to plan the foundation. He told Michael Hall: 'I am more inclined to the U.S. or Canada. Things are so slow moving here and England is in such a sorry state.' But he always returned to the central purpose of the work:

> I would like to see us establish a prayer centre and to have monks involved in the wider community life, e.g. as social or university workers as well as in pastoral work. Ideally then I think a small school, a parish and people of talent to work in the community generally would be the thing we should go for.

The details of the foundation are still hazy. So is Father John's strategy for convincing the authorities:

> How we will persuade our respective superiors [at Ealing and at St Anselm's] is another matter. But persuade them we will have to as the lack of hope in the present situation has to be turned around.

Then, before mid-September, came the good news. Father Bob Harris wrote that Bishop Crowley would like Father

John to telephone him when he came to Montreal. Father John could scarcely contain his excitement: 'I am on my way!' he wrote to Michael Hall, suggesting the news deserved a celebration, 'get in some Buchanan 12 years old and *decent* soda!' Besides arranging a trip to Washington, where he would speak to the community at St Anselm's (his first visit since losing the abbatial election a year before), Father John had agreed to give a series of talks on meditation to the Trappist community at the renowned Gethsemani Abbey (home for so long to Thomas Merton) in Kentucky. Two days later, on 13 September, he wrote to Michael Hall again: 'I have fixed up a meeting with the English-speaking Bishop in Montreal – keep this strictly *sub-sigillo*.' Another letter at the end of September nails down the important meeting in Montreal: 'I have an appointment in Montreal on the 23rd [of October] with Bishop Crowley, the Auxiliary for English affairs. I will make an appointment with him for my return too after I have talked with you.'

Bishop Crowley, a personable, progressive member of the Canadian Conference of Catholic bishops, readily agreed to see Father Main. He gave Father Harris his personal address card saying, 'Have Father John come to see me at the residence.' That is what John Main did after a brisk walk on Saturday morning, October 23rd from the Kruitwagens' house where he was staying. This initial meeting between Bishop Crowley and Father John occurred at a time of political unrest in Quebec. A bitter provincial election campaign was going on, and just three weeks later the first separatist government would be elected under the dynamic leadership of René Lévesque, a government committed to taking Quebec out of the Canadian federal system. Many people in Quebec, especially English-speaking people in Montreal were concerned. Bishop Crowley spoke of this concern indirectly to Father Main:

I shared with him my desire to bring to our city various religious communities, each of which might deepen and enrich the spiritual life of our priests and people with a sense of stability at a time of great political and social unrest in Quebec. Of course the monastic spirituality of the Benedictines would be a marvellous introduction to such an enterprise.

It was a beginning. Both men were pleased the meeting had gone so well. Father John brought the Bishop to visit the Kruitwagens. Hans Kruitwagen remembers how well the two men had got on: 'The visit with the Bishop opened John's eyes because the Bishop had so much faith in him. They really clicked.' After his meeting with Bishop Crowley, Father John found time for some socializing during his visit to Washington. On 10 November he wrote to his sister, Yvonne, in Dublin: 'Am staying with the Davitts ... very good form. Much social life – left the Irish Embassy at 1.30 Hrs in the morning! Tomorrow I go to the Trappists at Gethsemani in Kentucky.'

That simple line, 'Tomorrow I go to the Trappists at Gethsemani in Kentucky,' introduced one of the most important experiences on John Main's spiritual pilgrimage. A day or so after arriving at Gethsemani, he wrote a remarkable note date-lined 'Thomas Merton's Hermitage, Gethsemani, Kentucky, Nov. 13,' to his friend, Lady Lovat, a member of one of the first meditation groups at Ealing:

> ... I am here staying in Merton's hermitage out in the woods beyond Gethsemani. It is quite extraordinary how solitude brings everyone so close. I have just celebrated the most loving Mass of my life in Merton's little chapel. You were all so close to me as I prayed for you and all your family.
>
> My purpose in coming here was to talk to the Community about prayer, but in fact I have learnt so much myself while I have been here.

Why did John Main, normally so reticent and controlled when it came to his emotions, describe a wave of love washing over him in Merton's hermitage? What was it that John Main learned at Gethsemani? Obviously he learned more about himself and he acquired a deeper understanding of what Merton had been trying to do. Both men were on the pilgrimage, both had opted for the journey within. As with most travellers there were similarities and differences. As a young civil servant, John Main had made contact with the rich spiritual tradition of the East in Malaya. Through much of his monastic life and most dramatically at the end of it, Thomas Merton was seeking in the East. Is there any doubt that Merton's search for Eastern monastic traditions and his attempt to relate them to Western Christianity, made it easier for John Main to talk about the same journey in a different way?

As he tramped through the valley at Gethsemani on to the low knob where Merton's hermitage shone in the evening sun, John would remember that a long time ago Thomas Merton had stayed for a time in Ealing. John Main also knew that Thomas Merton had shared his concern about the future of monasticism. As Merton's biographer, Michael Mott, notes:

> ... even before he entered the monastery in 1941 he had pondered the question of how freedom to strive to be a saint might be aided by one religious structure, blocked by another. In 1956 and 1957, the question he was trying to ask was: What is the ideal structure for a monastery in our time?

In many respects, John Main was asking the same question. The question stayed with Main as it did with Merton. During a portion of 1952 Merton was physically ill. His physician, a Dr Law, was concerned about his condition. During that summer Dr Law was advising Merton to found an order because 'it was useless to introduce something new in the Trappists'. At the end of 1952, Dr Law's advice became stronger: 'Don't wait thirty years: go *now*.' Thomas Merton never founded a new order. Neither did John Main. But later Father John was to establish a new foundation that rebalanced the structures of the monastery as they related to prayer and work and their respective priorities.

For both monks, the Trappist and the Benedictine, monastic structures, however important, were there only to facilitate the growth of love. Both spoke against a deformed love. Father John often warned about 'objectifying' the other person in the relationship, making him or her (or God) an object to be used. In one of the most important passages he wrote on human love, Merton says:

> In the mystery of social love there is found the realization of 'the other' not only as one to be loved by us, so that we may perfect ourselves, but also as one who can become more perfect by loving us. The vocation to charity is a call not only to love but to *be loved*. The man who does not care at all whether or not he is loved is ultimately unconcerned about the true welfare of the other and of society. Hence we cannot love unless we also consent to be loved in return.

The reciprocal flow of love, contemporary monastic structures, these and other discussions always led back to the subject of prayer. And it is precisely in their prayer that Thomas Merton and John Main are most stimulating and rewarding. Both men were deeply read in John Cassian and the monastic tradition. (Interestingly too, both shared a love for the religious poetry of William Blake.) There is a suggestion in his biography that Merton sometimes used a mantra in his prayer: ' . . . he practised yoga breathing exercises or said the Jesus Prayer. . . '. Earlier in his life Merton considered that contemplative, imageless prayer was only for the few. Later he came to believe, what John Main had always taught, that a type of contemplation was accessible to ordinary people. As he progressed in his prayer life Merton was moving toward imageless prayer. He made more frequent reference to a line from a prayer he had once written for Our Lady: 'Teach me to go to the country beyond words and beyond names.' By 1968, according to his biographer, 'Thomas Merton had become an existential contemplative. This meant only that he had discovered the authentic journey and much of it would have to be made in silence.'

As he made ready for his final journey in the early fall of 1968, Thomas Merton's writing about the interior life resembled what John Main was teaching a few years later. In 1968 Merton wrote:

> Our real journey in life is interior; it is a matter of growth, deepening and of an ever greater surrender to the creative

action of love and grace in our hearts. Never was it more necessary for us to respond to that action.

Both shared the insight that human spirituality is not something to be discovered at the end of a treasure hunt. Rather the elements of the spiritual life are there all the time; they only require to be uncovered. And so, like John Main, Thomas Merton (often so turbulent in his own emotional life), realized that interior unity did not have to be created. As he said in a remarkable passage in Calcutta a few days before his death:

> . . . . the deepest level of communication is not communication but communion. It is wordless. It is beyond words, and it is beyond concept. Not that we discover a new unity. We discover an older unity . . . we are already one. But we imagine that we are not. And what we have to recover is our original unity. What we have to be is what we are.

John Main had always taught that meditation, practised with faith and perseverance, would permit the real self to develop, unified and unfragmented.

These similarities are not meant to suggest there were no differences of emphasis and approach in the matter of prayer between the two. Merton wrote a great deal about prayer; he wrote rather little about his personal prayer life or how he went about it. Main was writing about his own prayer most of the time. Merton was more of a writer; Main more the man of action. Physical place was more important to Merton than to Main. There was a good deal more of Merton's personality in his writings, about every subject from yoga to nuclear war. Main's writings, almost exclusively stressing Christian meditation, seemed to transcend his personality.

If there were a difference between Merton and Main on prayer, it related not to its nature but to the way of praying. John Main left a formal teaching about *how* to pray. Thomas Merton did not. The story of Abbot Isaac and the two young men who wanted to learn about prayer is relevant here. Thomas Merton, like Abbot Isaac initially, often spoke eloquently about prayer ('My prayer is then a kind of praise rising up out of the centre of Nothing and Silence'); John

Main, like Abbot Isaac later, developed a teaching, the continual repetition of the mantra, that gradually turned the meditator away from the illusions of the material world to a participation, in silence and in faith, in the unique prayer of Jesus to the Father present in the human heart.

This was the teaching and the way of prayer that Dom John articulated so effectively at Gethsemani in mid-November 1976, almost eight years after Thomas Merton's tragic death. Is it any wonder Father John was so moved by his experience there? He knew Thomas Merton had done so much, in his life and in his writings, to make so many people think about prayer, so many people want to pray. Father John also knew that Merton, more than any other, had blazed a path to the East, a path that had helped John Main's own pilgrimage. There can be little doubt that, when Father John stood in silence at the altar of Merton's hermitage, he understood the other pilgrim who had arrived with the Master. And the experience of talking with the monks at Gethsemani became a turning point for John Main, a compelling motive to pursue his own journey, to clarify his own teaching on prayer and to speak about it to anyone who wanted to listen.

Perhaps the memory of Merton gave Father John's conferences on prayer to Merton's old community at Gethsemani an added focus and clarity. (Later they would constitute his first publication on prayer called simply *Christian Meditation, the Gethsemani Talks*.) Father John gave the Gethsemani Trappists a simple description of prayer:

> ... as I understand it, all Christian prayer is a growing awareness of God in Jesus. And for that growing awareness we need to come to a state of undistraction, to a state of attention and concentration – that is, to a state of awareness. And as far as I have been able to determine in the limitations of my own life, the only way that I have been able to find to come to that quiet, to that undistractedness, to that concentration, is the way of the mantra.

One of the conferences was devoted to questions from the monks. Not surprisingly most of the questions related to the mantra and distractions:

It is the way *par excellence* to handle distractions because the purpose of the one word is simply to bring your mind to peace, silence and concentration. Not to bring it to rest with holy thoughts alone but to transcend what we know as thought altogether. And the mantra . . . is like a plough that goes through your mind pushing everything else aside. . . .

Then the few days at Gethsemani were over and Father John told the Trappists, 'I have loved being with you . . . I shall always remember with great affection these days among you.' He had learned his teaching on the way of prayer must be pursued more urgently than ever. He had also learned, beyond any doubt, this was the work for the kingdom to which he was called to give the rest of his life, no matter how long or short it might be.

From Gethsemani Father John returned to Montreal for a second productive meeting with Bishop Crowley. The Bishop told Father John that Montreal's Archbishop Paul Grégoire was positive, and he added: 'I felt deeply that the power of contemplative prayer would become a part of Montreal's spiritual life. I assured Dom John that I would search out ways to provide for whatever community might come among us. . . .'

The search began immediately when the Bishop took Father John on a tour of an inner-city parish that might be suitable for a beginning. When Father John returned to London in late November he wrote to Michael Hall of the warm welcome he had received from Bishop Crowley and their discussion of a base but he added, 'Now comes the hard work of persuading our community to allow it and then persuading some people to come.'

John Main was right to anticipate difficulties at Ealing – some of them quite understandable: 'News is not good. There is a good deal of opposition to the foundation idea. . . .' Father John's critics argued that Ealing could not afford manpower for an experimental foundation whose probable failure would redound to the discredit of Ealing itself. John's friends felt he should stay to cope with Ealing's current problems and become abbot at the next elections. Some were lobbying that he take over as head of the school, a proposal that had little appeal for him. But John Main's Irish sense of fun saw the humour in the situation. If the school, why not the whole monastery? 'Like General de Gaulle I would be prepared to assume the powers of the Republic – preferably as an Apostolic Administrator – but only for a limited period.'

In fact, John Main's light-hearted invocation of General de Gaulle indicated his real hopes: they no longer centred on Ealing but on the foundation. Nor was he deterred by problems raised by Michael Hall: a radical separatist government in Quebec, language difficulties, extreme weather. Despite these problems ('I am sure there are others') ' . . . we have to start and we have to start somewhere and we have to start soon'. He was excited about the possibility of a parish in Montreal: ' . . . I believe we could transform [it] with imagination and drive and above all a personal commitment to prayer and to one another in a more twentieth-century vision of monasticism.' It is significant that in all the ups and downs leading to the foundation, two elements remain constant – the emphasis on prayer and on community. If anything, despite the delays and disappointments, his confidence in his own vision was growing stronger: 'Many here will be quite upset not to say furious but I see no other way of saving our monastic life and I remain firm that it is worth saving.' This is further evidence of John Main's commitment to his monastic vocation.

Despite many uncertainties, including the situation in Montreal (the plan for an inner-city parish had fallen through, but Bishop Crowley had invited him to fly to Montreal for further discussions), John Main's life, at its centre, remained serene. He was now meditating for three half-hour periods a day and he encouraged Michael Hall:

> Your news on saying the mantra quite delights me. Do keep things going. It will make a marvellous calm grow right at the centre. If you find yourself giving it up – listen to one of the talks again. It does take some time to get rooted.

But despite his equanimity at the centre, John Main was about to be tested by still another upheaval at Ealing related to the Montreal plan. The occasion was the annual visitation of Ealing by an outside Benedictine Superior. It revealed some deeply held differences about the Montreal venture. More seriously, a few days later, at the end of January, Abbot Rossiter informed Father John that he did not approve of Montreal and would not support it. He also added that Brother Laurence Freeman could not go. Father John was not deterred. He wrote immediately to Bishop Crowley:

> If we allow this visitation dust to settle for a couple of months you could then take the initiative by sending a formal invitation to make a foundation in the Diocese of Montreal to the Abbot. If you could do this I would then take up the advocacy of the foundation here. I hope . . . that you won't lose patience with us. The Spirit works in very strange ways and often when an idea like this is discussed for the first time it gets side-tracked but then a firm proposition that follows later is accepted. . . . Ever since meeting you my heart is attached to this foundation.

At the same time John Main wrote a few sentences to Michael Hall that revealed the inner certitude that was sustaining him:

> This is a very testing time for us all but I think that something very creative could come out of all this confusion and chaos. Only keep saying your mantra and staying quietly in the presence of the Spirit of him who raised Jesus from the dead and who will give new life to your mortal body. These moments of growth and transition are always painful but they do lead to greater awareness.

Indeed something creative was about to emerge from the 'confusion and chaos'. At the end of February John was writing 'that Francis is now showing some interest in the Montreal project'. There is no doubt Father John's formidable powers of persuasion were having their effect on the Abbot's doubts about the enterprise. He would later explain his doubts as Bishop Crowley recalls: 'The Abbot indicated a fear that the single-mindedness of Dom John had caused concern that there would be few if any vocations from such an enterprise.' By the beginning of March, Father John was able to write to Bishop Crowley: 'Our Abbot is now ready to consider making the foundation in Montreal. He has asked me to go to see you as soon as possible.'

Toward the end of March, Father John flew to Montreal, in the words of Bishop Crowley (both he and Archbishop Grégoire wrote to Abbot Rossiter supporting the Montreal foundation), 'to learn of the social climate, to speak with the clergy and the faithful, to feel out His sense of purpose before the commitment became a reality'. The visit was a success. On his last night in Montreal, at a meeting with the clergy, the Bishop remembers some priests asking why Father John was coming to a place so unstable, socially and politically, when many were debating leaving Quebec:

> Father John responded beautifully, for he spoke of the *stability* of the monastic tradition. He recalled how all the monks were either imprisoned or expelled from England, and yet the Benedictines remain in Great Britain today as a symbol of the lasting stability of their life of prayer and of their monastic tradition. It was this very spirit he wished to bring to Montreal. . . .

After his trip to Montreal Father John arrived in Ealing to more good news: 'We had our Council. An overwhelming majority in favour of Montreal . . . I leave for California on the 29th. If the proposal is adopted at the Chapter, I shall return by way of Montreal to finalize matters. . . .'

The Chapter approved. John stopped off in Montreal in May and initiated plans to purchase a house on Vendôme Avenue in the western English section of the city close to the downtown area.

Then Father John returned to Ealing to still another crisis. Although two or three monks (including Laurence Freeman) had expressed a desire to join Father John in the Montreal foundation, Abbot Rossiter now did not want any to go. For once, Father John expressed his exasperation to Michael Hall: 'Do you think it was all a ploy to unload me!!??' In fairness to Abbot Rossiter he was facing enormous pressure from many in the Community that Ealing Abbey could not afford to lose any monks to Montreal, certainly not promising people such as Laurence Freeman. Despite this last-minute complication, John Main did not lose his sense of perspective and humour. 'Would that all men', he wrote to Michael Hall, 'could have the same expansive, broad and generous vision that is our great grace! But we must trust – the Lord who surely afflicts those he loves.' In his own way the Lord delivered. After another of Father John's persuasive interventions, the Ealing Council decided to permit Brother Laurence Freeman to go to Montreal with Father John.

Whatever his critics at Ealing thought of the Montreal project, John Main saw it as an adventure. This was the image he used repeatedly during the thirty-day retreat he gave at Wimbledon in July before leaving for Montreal. He spoke about adventure and leadership. For John Main (drawing to some extent on Jung) there were two kinds of leaders: the heroic leader and the father figure. The heroic leader stimulates his fellows by his vision, his courage, his example; he opens horizons, develops creativity, calls to adventure. Alexander the Great was an heroic leader. So was St Benedict. On the other side was the father figure. The father figure protects the *status quo*; he thinks for his followers, he shows them safe paths, he protects them. Father John thought most modern American presidents and evangelical preachers were father figures. The father figure says we know enough already. The heroic leader says we have more to find out, the adventure is just beginning.

For John Main the adventure began when he and Laurence Freeman left London's Heathrow Airport for Montreal on 28 September 1977. There was a sense of exhilaration at going but a sense of sadness, too, at leaving. For despite the difficulties, Ealing and the monks of Ealing had nurtured John Main's commitment to the monasticism of St Benedict and had provided so many dear friends he would never forget. Several from the Ealing community came over to the Meditation Centre to say good-bye. Abbot Rossiter himself drove them to Heathrow. John Main always had a sharp sense of the pain of partings. As he once wrote to Sister Miriam Quigley, who prayed with him at Wimbledon, helped him pack his books for Montreal, and never dreamed she would never see him again, 'Every parting is a kind of death. We go out into the unknown leaving familiar places and familiar faces, leaving those we love.'

So it was for John Main that September day in 1977. His long journey begun with David and Eileen in London half a century before, through Kerry and Ballinskelligs, Westminster Choir School and the Jesuits at St Ignatius, Welwyn Garden City and Diana, the *Hornsey Journal*, the Royal Signals, the Canons Regular, Dublin and the law, Malaya and the Swami, the English Bar, a monk of Ealing, Catholic University and St Anselm's, Ealing again and the teaching of Christian Meditation: the long journey had become a pilgrimage, its destination now an historic house on a suburban street in a cosmopolitan city in the province of Quebec.

11

Beginning in Montreal

'The whole thing here is a complete leap in the dark.' That
was how Father John described the Montreal project, and
that was literally how it began. After their flight from London,
Father John and Brother Laurence Freeman arrived in the
evening at Mirabel Airport outside Montreal, in the rain and
in the dark. The man who had so much to do with their
coming, Bishop Leonard Crowley, was at the airport to meet
them.

The meeting almost ended in a fiasco. Father John had left
Ealing in a rush. T-shirts had been jammed into a bulging
brief-case secured with the only fastener at hand, the belt
from his trousers. This precarious arrangement withstood the
pressures of the transatlantic flight. Unfortunately, at Mirabel
airport, as Father John, beltless, stretched out his hand to
meet his new bishop, the bulging brief-case burst open.
Happily Father John's trousers held firm; so did his remarkable composure.

He would need all his composure as he began the new
enterprise in Montreal in the autumn of 1977. A week after
he arrived with Brother Laurence, living as guests of the
Ascension Parish in Westmount, Father John wrote to Father
Michael Hall:

> It is impossible to say what opportunities there will be for
> us or how the whole thing will take on. But basically I
> think the only important thing is that we are a group who
> want to pray together and to respond to the needs of the
> kingdom as they appear.

The needs of the kingdom, as they appeared, were mundane
indeed. They related to the house John Main had purchased,

with the Bishop's help (virtually the only money the two Benedictines had was in their pockets) on Vendôme Avenue in the municipality of Notre-Dame-de-Grâce near downtown Montreal. It was one of the historic Décarie houses, built by the descendants of Jean Décarie, who had come out from France about 1650 when Paul de Chomedey, Sieur de Maisonneuve, was trying to develop what would become the city of Montreal. But the house had fallen into a state of disrepair and there were other problems, as Father John explained to Lady Lovat about a month after arriving in Montreal: ' . . . we are still not able to get legal possession and wait, like orphans, on the doorstep'.

This was one of the first of many letters from Montreal to Rosamund 'Rosie' Lovat, a tall, reserved, regal woman with a loyal discretion that matched her generous heart. She became not only a strong supporter of the Montreal foundation but also a confidante to whom Father John turned for encouragement and reassurance. Not only her friendship but her commitment to meditation was a constant source of comfort to him: 'I can't tell you how delighted I was that so many of you really managed to understand the wonderful simplicity and richness of meditation. It is simply a matter of patient fidelity and a readiness for that full openness to the Lord.'

Simple but not easy. Already one of Father John's Benedictine friends was having second thoughts about the project he and Father John had discussed so often. In early October 1977 Father John wrote to Father Michael Hall in Washington:

I can well understand your reservations about leaving Washington and of course I must in no way encourage you to desert what you see as your responsibilities. I understand your dilemma well because I went through the same at Ealing over the years. It may be that you will come (because the circumstances are different) to a conclusion different from mine. But whatever your decision rest assured that I will respect and understand it. Whatever you do decide I hope that you will come and visit us here from time to time.

Father John also reiterated there were no guarantees in the Montreal situation and they would not be living in the lap of luxury:

> We shall be very poor! We have been given $57,000 in gifts and loans which will cover the cost of purchasing the house ($47,000) and some money for repairs and renovations. We will have to furnish from scrap and equip! We have $25,000 a year to live on, but the cost of living seems very high here and we will need to watch the way we spend. This I think will be a good thing for us all.

Bishop Crowley was responsible for the financial support of the new Benedictine foundation. The Bishop was very gratified by the generous response particularly of Quebec's religious communities, including the French ones. Even Abbot Rossiter, at a time when Ealing could ill spare the money, sent Father John an ample donation.

On 6 December, the plumbing fixed, the deeds signed and the electricity turned on, Father John and Brother Laurence moved into the old Décarie House at 3761 Vendôme Avenue just a few yards from the busy Côte-St-Antoine road. By this time two of the young people from the lay community at Ealing, John Westby and Pat Hawes, had come to help with the move and to join, at least temporarily, the fledgling foundation. Guests began to arrive, welcomed sometimes by Father John, paint brush in hand. The first meditation group, which had met that spring with Sister Eileen Byrne at St Ignatius parish, was now joined by others. Montrealers, in slowly increasing numbers, came to ask for instruction in Christian meditation, usually given by Father John on Monday and Tuesday evenings, followed by a meditation in silence. Plans were made for a newsletter to go out to meditators and, after being in Vendôme less than a month, Father John was writing to Rosie Lovat about plans for her first visit and the need for more space. But there was play as well as work:

> Some friends of mine came and took me off 'snow-shoeing' the other day – it was a sort of kidnap! But I enjoyed it immensely. We walked over a lake (frozen!) and through

some pine woods, all in about three feet of snow and the deepest silence you have heard – really inspiring. I made a resolution to go snow-shoeing whenever I can.

Then, as he often did in letters to Rosie Lovat and others, Father John returned to the subject of meditation and the prayer groups:

I am delighted you have joined Fr Vincent's group and I know that nothing will deflect you from fidelity to the simplicity of the mantra. Other teachers think it is useful to keep up the interest of the group with various things. I am sure that this is good provided it doesn't compromise the main issue. There is really nothing to be learned – nothing to experience or anything like that. It is simply a matter of realization – we must realize who we are – in Jesus. The rest is really so much froth – but people do get a bit restless if you merely repeat, 'Say your Mantra', and so teachers think of all sorts of other techniques and clever things to say and so on. The only thing is to open your heart to the love of the Lord Jesus and the only way I know to do it is to be simply faithful to the mantra day by day.

Father John was writing this letter at the end of 1977. It had been a bitter-sweet year for him – the excitement of the new foundation, the sadness of leaving Ealing where he had become a Benedictine monk, been ordained a priest and where he still had many friends. He was happy, at the year's end, to hear good news from Rosie about his old monastery: 'I am so glad that things are going well at Ealing. . . . It is often the case that things turn out that way. I think that my going made it possible. There is no doubt but that this is the Lord's doing.' 'I think that my going made it possible': no looking back in bitterness or regret at what might have been; but looking forward with enthusiasm to what would be.

In the first week of January 1978 he wrote to tell Michael Hall that more prayer groups would meet that week: 'At Ealing we went from five to two hundred in six months. I hope the expansion will be somewhat slower here.' The structure of the meetings was much the same as those at the Ealing Prayer Centre: 'an introductory talk, music, a half-hour meditating in silence together, the raising of questions or a discussion'. Early in the new year a small group of priests began meditating. By this time Father John was able to tell Michael Hall that the daily monastic regime was gradually being put in place: 'office, the Eucharist, work, three periods of silent meditation, recreation, music etc. No TV!' (Although he considered recreation important, Father John had concluded that, by and large, television was damaging to community life.) He described both the joy and the difficulty of the monastic schedule:

> We have now established our full round of monastic prayer and it has been a great joy to return to the regular life. . . . Of course we have our problems to get everyone entirely together, but the uniting factor is the commitment of everyone to the prayer together.

That relatively few people came to Vendôme in the early days did not seem to concern Father John. He never played the spiritual numbers game. Gradually more arrived to be taught Christian meditation (the Monday night talk) and to progress more deeply into it (the Tuesday night session). Before the prayer Father John spoke about meditation for about twenty minutes:

> Learning to meditate is the most practical thing in the world. You require only one quality when you begin. That is seriously to want to learn to meditate. The process is absolute simplicity. . . . You need to find a quiet place . . . and, having found it, you sit down. . . . When you are seated and are still, you close your eyes and then begin to repeat, interiorly and silently in your heart, the word Maranatha ('Come, Lord Jesus'). In some traditions this is called a 'mantra', in others, a 'Prayer phrase' or 'Prayer word' . . . [*Maranatha*] is an Aramaic word and its importance is both that it is one of the most ancient prayers there is and that it possesses the right sound to bring us to the silence and stillness necessary for meditation. . . . And that is all you need to know in order to meditate. You have a word, and you say your word, and you remain still.

When anyone asked Father John about progress in medi-

1   Eileen and David Main on their wedding day: 7 February 1920

2 The Main family in 1935: from left to right Alan, Diane, Douglas (John Main), Yvonne, Ian, Kitty

3 Douglas (John Main) in 1949 with his niece Anne-Marie Stanley

4 Swami Satyananda (1909-1961) as a young man

6 Diana Ernaelsteen in 1958 aged 23

5 Called to the Bar in 1960

7 The Meditation Centre at Ealing Abbey. Front row: second left Bernard
   Orchard OSB, centre John Main, second right Benedict O'Donohoe OSB.
   Back row: centre Laurence Freeman

8 The visit of H.H. The Dalai Lama to the
   Vendôme Priory in 1980. From left to right:
   Laurence Freeman, H.H. The Dalai Lama,
   John Main

9 John Main in 1982

10 John Main with Victor Dammertz, OSB, Abbot Primate of the Benedictine
    Confederation, in 1982

tation he would reply, with a smile, that the first 20 years were the most difficult. Nor did he ever suggest, or even imply, that meditators formed some kind of spiritual elite. He once referred to a Tuesday night group (including himself) as 'this motley crew' and he told Michael Hall, 'We are really a very ordinary group doing a very ordinary sort of job! As if you did not know.' During the early months of 1978, the outlines of 'the very ordinary group' at the Vendôme Priory were clearer. It comprised three levels: the monastic community, still only two, Father John himself and Brother Laurence Freeman; the lay community, then three young men from England and two women (a nurse, Pat Hawes, and Sister Eileen Byrne); and finally the meditation groups.

During this early period of the foundation Father John was under considerable pressure in terms of space, financing and the scarcity of monastic help. There is a hint of this in a letter to Michael Hall. Apparently some of the Benedictines in Ealing, whom Father John had been counting on, now might not come. A hint, too of the loneliness John Main occasionally felt, so far from all his old friends:

> We don't get much news from Washington. . . . Do write when you have a moment and give all your news. I hear very little from Ealing and so have little word of them. We hope that Vincent will come to join us here but the Abbot seems a little uncertain about it.

Presently Father John's fears about manpower from Ealing were confirmed: 'I hear from Ealing that Vincent will not now be coming, and Vincent suggests that no one will be spared. So we will have to work on that supposition.' Father John adjusted to what must have been a major disappointment with remarkable resiliency: 'I have cancelled all my engagements in Europe during the summer. I had thought Vincent would be here and that it would be good for him to be on his own with the group but now I must think again. I am very pleased.'

One friend in London did not forget Father John nor his work in Montreal. After her marriage in the French Church off Leicester Square, the church that once meant so much to them both, Diana Ernaelsteen (Searle) graduated in medicine, began to practise, and had three children, the first a thalidomide baby. For a long time she and John Main did not meet. Then, when he was still in Washington, Father John's special friendship with Diana revived. He was delighted, as he explained in a letter to his friends from Malayan days, David and Jane Akers-Jones:

> Do you remember Diana? We once had lunch together in London. We met again during the summer [1973] . . . and have been in constant correspondence ever since – she a happy wife and mother and me a happy monk – but I think made happier by discovering an old love that had not dimmed over the years. I am getting sentimental so I will close.

It is typical of John Main that this flash of emotion, flickering like sheet-lightning, is quickly brought under control. But their love had not dimmed and Father John was happier knowing it had not. In one of her birthday letters to Father John in Washington, Diana (who continued to live in Welwyn Garden City) reminded him he once carried her on his shoulders. He remembered:

> Thank you for the lovely birthday card. . . . So it's shoulders! Amazing that you should remember that so clearly. Years later I carried another (somewhat bigger) girl on my shoulders and as a result suffer from chronic fibrositis! I often think that shoulder trouble was the beginning of my flight to the monastery – being too flighty I suppose.

When Father John returned to England in 1974, Diana was working primarily in children's medicine. Shortly after his return Father John visited Diana and her family in their home. On that occasion he discussed his plans for a new prayer centre at Ealing with Diana's husband, Geoffrey. Later he wrote to Diana:

> What an enormous pleasure it was to see you the other day – a very happy day. I so enjoyed the walk in the woods and playing with the children – I suppose I have never grown up!!!
> I was very grateful too for my very brief conversation

with Geoffrey. It was most useful to have his comments on my proposed community of prayer. . . .

Some time in the future I am thinking of getting a few people together to discuss the question of prayer as a practical reality – maybe Geoffrey and you might come along. It would be refreshing to have a view that was not inspired by the commitment to the Christian revelation.

Father John's leaving for Montreal saddened Diana, but they continued writing. She was interested in the new foundation and Father John (of course she still called him Douglas) gave her a progress report in the spring of 1978:

Starting this place from scratch has been a great challenge. We haven't really got airborne yet but we are on the way. We have a very nice old house that was quite a wreck when we moved in and now we are beginning to get it straight. . . . I am so sorry that we didn't have an opportunity to meet before I left.

I like the life here in North America. There seems to be so much more initiative and innovativeness in the people. But I suppose I am basically a displaced person, a refugee.

In March 1978, two young men, Tom Abraham and Nicholas Wardropper, came from London to join the lay community. Abbot Francis Rossiter himself came over for a visit in June. He enjoyed his visit and the warm hospitality at Vendôme, as Father John told Rosie Lovat: 'The Abbot's visit was a great success. We had very little time to prepare anything for him but I think he got quite a fair idea of our aims and work. He seemed very rested and peaceful when he was going.' About this time too Father John was delighted to hear from Rosie about her own meditation group. He replied:

It is really wonderful that you have been able to start this group. The quietest room possible will be the best. . . . Try to give them something from your own experience each time. It need only be a sentence or two – the message is so simple – 'keep to the mantra'. You will find that this is the biggest stumbling block – especially to devout Catholics and Religious. Never argue – and never lose your cool! Just repeat that this is the teaching and that this is your

115

experience . . . make sure you keep the simplicity of the mantra. I know you will. There is however such a temptation to dress the whole thing up into strange and esoteric garbs.

By the summer of 1978, Father John's vision of the kind of community he wanted to build in Montreal was emerging. He referred to this in a letter to Rosie Lovat in July:

Our plans go ahead here and we are now coming within sight of our dream – that is a community of monks, sisters, lay community and married people and families – all joined together by meditation – obviously at different levels of commitment but each with a growing commitment.

One of the most exciting and revolutionary elements in Father John's fresh vision of community was the role of lay people, both those living inside and outside the community itself. As the community developed so would the active participation of the laity, single or married. This would be one of Father John's contributions to modern monasticism – a community life where, for example, the oblates (those with a special commitment to prayer and the office) were not just a passive guild of pious women but a group of people who formed an integral part of the monastic community, its prayer life and its activities, some of which they initiated. In a real sense the monastery was to be the centre of a growing family linked by strong spiritual bonds. This was a vital and developing monasticism – flexible, prayerful, vitally connected to the real world. Father John described the thrust of the Montreal experiment in *Letters from the Heart*:

In this society of entertainment and spiritual eclecticism, but marked, too, by so much genuine concern for a true experience of absolute value, it seemed to me that the monastic witness of the kind we were making in Montreal was of supreme importance – simply to prove to a culture built to such an extent on 'conditional discipleship' that only the *absolute* commitment can bring the liberation they seek and so often do not find.

A part of the 'monastic witness' in Montreal that most

116

encouraged Father John was the number of people who came to Vendôme regularly to participate in the prayer life and share meals with the community. They formed, in a sense, an extension of the lay community. One of these was a young salesman in his twenties, Paul Lafontaine. He came to the Priory for the office and meditation three times a day and shared most of his meals with the community. He and Father John became friends, partly through their common interest in music. Paul was astonished at Father John's appreciation and knowledge of music: 'He was a musician's musician, with a very good ear and a pleasing tone.' Paul Lafontaine recounts an interesting theory Father John had developed about Baroque music:

> He would point out how there existed, in Baroque music, a relationship between the musical pulsings and the duration of a breath in a human at relaxation. Thus the music corresponded to a rhythmic harmony in humans, making it suitable for relaxation, attentive appreciation and even digestion. He felt that the Haydn Symphonies and the Mozart Concertos were ideal vehicles to listen to at meal times given their structure and length, about 25 minutes.

Music, meditation, talks – Father John also made time for an extensive correspondence. An old Irish friend, Monsignor Tom Fehily, pastor of the delightfully named parish of Castle-knock-Porterstown-Clonsilla, wrote to him about organizing meditation meetings. He replied:

> 1. In regards the format of your meetings, we have found that the talk time should not be more than 15 minutes and ideally only 5–7 or so. I think the rest of your format is good. Assemble – listen to talk – meditate – discuss. I think it important to stress that the discussion should not be on 'what happened' but on more practical things like good time, good reading, good posture, etc. etc. As regards reading. In the initial stages the less the better. Advise against getting into too many technicalities.
> 2. About teaching others. As long as you are scrupulously honest and only try to teach what you know and don't

117

mind saying 'I don't know the answer to that', I would say start a group wherever you can. You can always use some tapes for the initial stages. The important thing is to meditate. I think a weekly meeting of the group is of enormous help if it can possibly be managed.

It's very good I think to be in touch with a Community and feel absolutely welcome to be in touch with ours. Anytime you want to write or anyone wants to come and stay (The Maple Leaf fare is quite cheap!) you will always be welcome. . . . The Community dimension is important because it does provide a point of reference for you that gives confidence to your group. This is the idea behind our newsletters. . . . Our work is expanding quite rapidly here and in all sorts of places in the world.

One of the places where the work was expanding was London, and one of the people there whose interest meant much to Father John was Diana. He was surprised to learn she had listened to his meditation tapes: 'How strange that you should have listened to the tapes.' He tells her he hopes to see her and her family early in 1979: 'So you are 43. I can hardly imagine it. Of course I am nearly sixty myself!' (This was a typical John Main exaggeration; he was in fact 52). Then he recommended a book to Diana: 'You must read *100 Years of Solitude*, Gabriel Garcia Marquez. It is a wild tale of imagination and reality that is one of the great books of all times.' Then, as he often did with Diana, Father John described some aspect of the outdoors they both loved so much, this time an autumn tree outside the driveway of the old Décarie house on Vendôme:

It has been staggeringly beautiful here for the last weeks. A very slow Fall with the leaves getting more and more unbelievable – reality is really so much more fantastic than fantasy – or as someone said Nature does really imitate art. We have a tree at the entrance to our drive that has looked like an old lady growing gracefully and more and more beautifully old – starting with full reds going to light browns, then to golds and then to frail spun gold.

By the close of the first full year at the Vendôme Priory, the structure of the new foundation, still fragile, was becoming more firm. At the end of 1978, the Priory received its first oblate, Rosie Lovat. The big problem, as the new year began, was not lack of activity but lack of space.

After a round of talks and retreats on meditation in the early part of 1979, in England, Scotland and Ireland (where he had a short visit with his family), Father John returned home to sad news. Diana wrote to say that her father, Harry Ernaelsteen, had died. When John lived with the Ernaelsteens at the beginning of the war, he had grown fond of Diana's father:

> Harry's death must have been so hard for you as I know how much he relied on you. I loved him very much – he was really such an important figure in my life. Only during these last days have I realized how much. I think he gave me almost all the confidence I have! Isn't it strange and I don't think I have known that clearly all my life. I shall always keep him in my heart and daily remember him in the Mass that meant so much to him in recent years. I think it must have been that I saw his faults clearer than my father's, and his faults somehow made him greater in my eyes – there was something generous there that was very attractive.

It was almost forty years since Harry Ernaelsteen had told John Main he could be anybody he wanted to be, do anything he wanted to do, preferably neatly dressed. John Main had never forgotten. In her reply to his letter about her father's death, Diana took up the notion of human faults. She did not perceive people having 'faults' so much as their having a continuum of qualities that would be perceived differently by different people. Nor did she think it fair to assess individual qualities; the whole man must be considered and the sum total of his contribution. As usual, John Main found Diana's letter both stimulating and moving. He speculates about their long-lived mutual empathy and understanding. Was it owing to his mother and Diana's grandmother meeting and becoming close friends in Belgium before World War I:

> I was so delighted to get your letter and very moved as I

read it. It is so curious that we share so much in spirit. Could it have been those early genetic meetings in the pre-first-World-War Brussels that gave us such an affinity? But whatever it is it is extraordinary.

Perhaps it was environment – a people is made a people by its early memory – and I suppose we were both in our own way affected by those brief years or was it months in W.G.C. [Welwyn Garden City].

Whatever the explanation, the affection of those teen-aged years at W.G.C. ripened into love and then into a selfless service to others, Diana, a doctor in the practice of healing, John, a monk teaching meditation, a service that subsumed their own love but did not extinguish it.

During these early months trying to develop the community at Vendôme nothing gave Father John more encouragement and stimulus than hearing about meditation groups elsewhere. He wrote to Rosie Lovat responding to some of her questions about prayer:

Your union and communion ideas are perfectly sound, 'How can you say you love God who you cannot see if you do not love your neighbour who you can see?' (St John).

Love of neighbour is the perfect preparation for prayer (loss of self in God) and prayer is the perfect preparation for love of neighbour (loss of self in others). It is sternness and the ability to encounter it without fear that is the beginning of love.

Then he referred to one of his favourite thoughts from Teilhard de Chardin: 'Union differentiates . . . the more we love (ourselves) in the other the more we become ourselves.' He also told Rosie about the Anglican bishop, Henry Hill, who would later join the community and become another of its first oblates: 'We had a delightful Anglican bishop with us for nearly three weeks – the Bishop of Ontario. He fitted in perfectly and loved meditating with us four times a day':

The wonderful thing about meditation is that it prevents all fooling around with religion. If you really want to say your mantra then you can harbour [no] resentment and irritation in your heart. That is not to say that you won't feel it! At least from time to time – but as soon as it presents itself it must be banished. The beauty of it is that it is banished not by our will but by God's Love.

Father John had enjoyed good health in Montreal. But a medical problem emerged in the late summer of 1979. After giving a retreat to the sisters of the Congregation of Notre Dame at Mabu in Nova Scotia, followed by a brief sea-shore holiday, he returned to the Priory. He first noticed pains in his lower abdomen in September. They became worse. A doctor at the Queen Elizabeth Hospital diagnosed cancer of the upper bowel.

It was decided to operate immediately. Father John wanted to tell some of his closest friends himself. He telephoned Rosie Lovat at her home in Scotland and followed the call with a letter:

How lovely it was talking to you on the 'phone'. I was so sorry to give you bad news but I didn't want you just to hear it third-hand.

It is apparently quite a serious operation – the doctors say – serious but not grave!! [No matter what the circumstances Father John could seldom resist his proclivity for punning].

. . . It's strange how suddenly this illness has developed! I haven't quite got used to the idea of it yet. But I feel very calm and am totally open to God's will whether it be life or death. I hope I will be able to say the mantra throughout the uncomfortable bits of it. Keep me in your heart.

The beauty of meditation is the real simplicity it leads you to – a real capacity to respond to what IS.

The doctors operated on 9 October. They pronounced the operation a complete success. One person, who had been increasingly concerned by Father John's long silence, was Diana in Welwyn Garden City, then practising community paediatrics in Hertfordshire:

Douglas had not written for a long while. I found myself awake several nights running, acutely anxious about him and with him in my thoughts I then wrote a (relatively) angry letter, in funny vein, saying that only a brain tumour would do as an excuse for not writing.

Although he was just out of hospital, Father John replied by post-card:

> Dearest Diana,
>
> This is just to give you a bad conscience!! But not too bad!! But I am just recovering (2 days out of hospital) from major surgery. Was quite ill for a few weeks. Growth in bowel – seems to be a great success – no infection in lymph nodes. Will write as soon as I am stronger. Much love. Douglas.

He then added a typical remark, 'Really enjoyed your letter. Sorry I can't match the invective!' In response to this card, and for the first and only time, Diana telephoned Father John in Montreal:

> I got through to him immediately and his feelings, usually so carefully covered (indeed virtually *always*) were revealed by a strained voice, 'So you do care after all.' He made light of the hard times in his life and wrote of the successes and highlights.

Unfortunately, because he was still recuperating, Father John was unable to attend one of the 'highlights' of 1979, Brother Laurence Freeman's solemn profession as a Benedictine. Bishop Crowley was present as, indeed, was Abbot Rossiter who made the long journey from England. The Abbot visited Father John, whose doctors advised him to spend a few weeks in the warm South to regain his strength. Just before leaving Father John wrote to Diana for her birthday:

> Forgive my prolonged silence, but I have put all my energy into recovering from the surgery. It seems to have worked. I am now back to full health! Blood – all sets of tests – including haemo or is it heamo-globins or whatever, all counting perfectly, pressure fine and weight back to a somewhat portly 190 lbs which is what it always has been for several years now.

So in the first week of January 1980, Father John,

accompanied by Brother Laurence, flew to the Bahamas, to stay at St Augustine's Benedictine Monastery in Nassau for a month. It was a sunny way to leave the shadow of illness, and as he stood on a hilltop in the sunshine looking out at the sea, Father John, now sporting a light grey beard could feel his health swiftly reviving. And, as he wrote to Rosie Lovat, he enjoyed the sea and the sun: 'It is quite lovely here. Very silent – very remote from the tourist part. A small Community (no one over five feet) but very friendly and welcoming.'

Still there was work to do. While Brother Laurence did the editing, Father John wrote the Introduction to the first series of Newsletters from the Priory, later published as *Letters from the Heart*. And he wrote to Rosie about one of his basic themes, the distinction between illusion and reality:

There is the true self (Atman) which is Christ, in him, with him and through him we are in God (Brahman). There is the false self (Ego) which has no reality and does not exist – it is only illusion. The false self burns away and gives way to the true self in the fire of Divine Love who is Christ. 'My me is God; neither do I know myself save in him' (Catherine of Genoa). In other words there is only God – he is the one supreme reality. We can only know him with his own self-knowledge which is the life of the Trinity. Our intention is to leave illusion – to leave unreality – God's call is to leave the 'I' and become 'me'. We must all become 'me'. I hope that clarifies rather than obfuscates.

After what he described as 'a splendid rest', Father John and Laurence returned to Vendôme to an intense round of engagements. They flew to Victoria, British Columbia, at the invitation of Bishop Remi de Roo to give a week's series of talks in the cathedral. The crowds were large and enthusiastic. Back home the whole community was busy preparing for Laurence's ordination. As Father John wrote to Rosie: 'Laurence is really very excited but playing it cool!' In June in the lovely chapel of the motherhouse of the sisters of the Congregation of Notre Dame, Bishop Leonard Crowley ordained Laurence Freeman OSB to the priesthood. This was the climax of Laurence's successful studies in theology at the University of Montreal.

At this time too Father John's writings on meditation were having a wider influence. He explained to Rosie:

> I had a lovely letter from the Archbishop of Canterbury saying how much he had enjoyed 'The Other Centeredness of Mary'. He said that he was due to preach at Walsingham soon and that it had stimulated him in preparing his sermon. It was a very warm and friendly letter.

Now it was time for Father John's usual trip overseas to give retreats, days of recollection, talks to meditation groups and enjoy a brief visit with his family in Ireland. He wrote to Rosie in July:

> Kylemore Abbey where I gave the first retreat is a lovely place. The nuns were very delightful – very simple like children some of them. One of them said to me 'And where Father did you get that grand English accent and coming from the depths of the County Kerry?!'
>
> Some of them I think got the message of meditation but by no means all. I am now with a group of Dominican Sisters and I have the impression that they may be more on the wave-length.

Still, his expectations were modest:

> Ireland was damply beautiful and I enjoyed the two retreats which were really restful for me. In each of the Communities there were two or three who really understood and who will tread the pilgrimage to the end. This is a great grace.

After his return to Montreal in mid-July, the Priory was inundated with guests. If some tried his patience, they did not squelch his humour. He told Rosie, 'We are full of guests and I have to spend much time with them as they are all so anxious for an immediate encounter with the Absolute!' There is also a word about suffering:

> . . . let me tell you what I feel about suffering. There are situations in life that are so unbearable that only terrible

violence seems able to bring relief and deliverance. The Cross itself is the archetypal instance. When such violence seizes hold of people they act only out of the narrowness of their violence and not out of the fullness of their humanity. Hence the 'Father forgive them they know not what they do'.

Forgiving really does mean unremembering – letting go all remembrance of the violence and allowing only the full humanity to be.

At the same time he was writing to Rosie Lovat, Father John was also keeping up a large correspondence with other meditators around the world. He wrote to one in Ireland:

I am so delighted to hear that meditation has meant so much to you. There is great healing in it. As you become more quiet and go deeper into the mystery of God you begin to understand that the mystery is of the infinite depths of the Divine Love which is absolutely all-sufficing. You begin to understand that you don't have to live out of your own limited resources but out of the infinite compassion of God.

And with typical John Main enthusiasm he added, 'Isn't it absolutely wonderful!'

What was also 'absolutely wonderful', at a different level, was the news about a new site for the Priory (which the previous summer had transferred its affiliation from Ealing to Mount Saviour in New York State.) With the assistance of Montreal businessman, Jean Prieur, Father John started to search for a larger property. Then, almost miraculously, came the possibility of acquiring one of the most spectacular mansions in a city famous for them.

The story of how the McConnell estate became the Benedictine Priory is an astonishing one. On his way back from a trip to England, Father Laurence met a middle-aged couple on their way to Montreal. They seemed interested in meditation so he told them about the Priory. Later, their daughter spoke about Father John and meditation to a friend, David Laing, son of Mrs Peter (Kit) Laing who, in turn, was the daughter of the late J. W. McConnell, a prominent

Montrealer who had once owned one of Canada's most respected newspapers, the *Montreal Star*.

David Laing, an engaging young man with nervous problems, began going to the Priory to meditate. Later he had several discussions with Father John who gave him some clear-cut advice. David learned that the Priory desperately needed more space. He casually remarked to Father John that his family owned a house in downtown Montreal. (Jean Prieur had also learned that the house was available.) Just as casually Father John went with David Laing to look at the house with its palatial terraces, turrets, court yards and tennis courts. It was situated in a wooded estate above Pine Avenue half-way up the magnificent Mount Royal with a breath-taking view of Montreal down to the St Lawrence River and beyond to the green hills of Vermont. This was the McConnell mansion (with its eighteen bedrooms and a spacious coach-house), one of the half dozen most celebrated homes in Montreal.

Father John realized immediately the house would be ideal as a Priory because of its secluded environs and central location. But was it a real possibility? Father John invited 'Kit' Laing for tea at Vendôme. To his delight and surprise (the McConnells were from a staunch Protestant background), he learned that 'Kit' Laing favoured her old home (now used mainly for social events) becoming a Benedictine Priory. But she was just one member (albeit the president) of the foundation that controlled the estate. What would they say? In their discussions one gentleman asked Father John, 'And how long have you been around?' 'About 1,500 years,' Father John replied.

Then he wrote to Rosie to explain another difficulty raised by the foundation, though one not shared by 'Kit' Laing herself:

> Out of the blue we have been offered a very large house on Pine Avenue (downtown) as a gift. Unfortunately they were about to sell the gardens for a considerable sum to a developer. As this would make the house useless for us I told them that I couldn't really accept the House for the Community unless they gave me the land too! They are

now considering this and I am waiting to hear from them. It would be a very good interim solution.

It was a risky response. No grounds, no house. But it revealed more about John Main than it did about houses. He knew what he wanted. And whether it was a house or a commitment to meditation he wanted all or nothing. The risk was worth it. The McConnell mansion, grounds and all (including even the butler) became a Benedictine Priory in June. The plans were to move in during the fall. After so much excitement over the new house, Father John went off in early September to give a meditation retreat in St Louis, Missouri, where 'the weather was hot – 100 degrees F. each day'. For someone who had never been that keen on sport, he took drastic measures to cool off:

> After [the retreat] was over I went down to visit some friends in Southern Missouri who have a lovely house on the North Fork River, a tributary of the Missouri River. While there I did some white water canoeing! It was great fun shooting the rapids at high speed – we only came out once! You soon learn at that speed.

Shortly after his return to the Priory from St Louis, Father John was delighted to welcome a new member to the monastic community. Paul Geraghty, a young solicitor, 26 years old, from Liverpool, had spent about six months at the Vendôme Priory in 1978. For some years he had been thinking of the monastic life. As early as 1975 Paul had gone to see Abbot Francis Rossiter at Ealing. The Abbot suggested he talk with Father John who was guest-master at the time. Later, in 1975, Paul joined Father John's meditation groups at Ealing. After his stay at Vendôme in 1978, he returned to Liverpool to practise law, then, when family responsibilities permitted, he returned in October 1980, a shy, extremely capable and like-able young man, a solid addition to the monastic community. He arrived just in time for the big move and also to help welcome the most notable visitor of the year, the Dalai Lama, spiritual leader of the Tibetan Buddhists.

Father John, who had done so much to enrich the prayer life of the West by his personal experience of prayer in the

East, was delighted to invite the Dalai Lama, while on a Canadian tour, to the Benedictine Priory. He was also pleased that the Dalai Lama and most of his entourage shared the mid-day Office, responded to the prayers and meditated with the community for half an hour in silence. For Father John, this silent prayer of those from the East with their brothers and sisters of the West, had profound significance:

> We meditated together in absolute openness to love and to the Lord of love. We were not trying to convert one another. Our challenge as Christians is not to try to convert people around us to our way of belief but to love them, to be ourselves living incarnations of what we believe, to live what we believe and to love what we believe.

There was only one jarring note. As Father John walked out of the meditation room after the half hour of silence one of the Dalai Lama's security people, a worried look on his face, grabbed his arm and asked warily, 'Say, what was going on in there?'

After the visit of the Dalai Lama, all hands were mobilized to help with the move. Rosie Lovat was planning to come over for a visit (as she usually did a couple of times a year). Father John wrote to her:

> Just to let you know that the donation of the house is now complete. The Board met last week and confirmed that they would give us everything – house, land and furnishings. They have given us November 1st as our date of entry. So you will be able to be with us as we start this new chapter in our history.

The beginning of 'this new chapter in our history', the move itself, helped by many friends from the Priory, went off smoothly and was embellished by a typical John Main incident. Father John, like the lay community and other helpers, was wearing working clothes. A man living nearby was watching this moving crew in action. He asked whom they worked for. Father John replied, 'The National Moving Company.' Could they move a sideboard to his nearby home in Westmount? They could and they did. Could they move another piece of furniture downstairs? Father John replied they had to get back for Vespers ('which apparently he thought were some kind of Italian motorcycle').

So by early November, the Benedictine 'National Moving Company' had the community ensconced in its new Priory on Pine Avenue. By now three monastic novices, including two Americans, had joined. It had been a busy and fruitful year for the Montreal Priory.

Early in 1981 Father Laurence went for an extended trip to visit and encourage the prayer groups overseas. He stopped in Germany to speak with other meditation groups on his way home. Father John went to California (one of his favourite places) in February to speak to his largest crowd ever. He refers to this in a letter to Diana:

> I have been postponing writing to you so that I could send you a worthy closely argued treatise on reflections on life now that I am in the mid-fifties! But in case I never get around to that I am sending you this brief bearer of loving tidings.
>
> Life has been full. Had my first experience of talking to a large crowd – 8,000 – in the Anaheim Convention Centre outside Los Angeles. After that took part in some 'conventions' in San Diego. I can't understand why everyone in the world doesn't live it up in Southern California.

In the spring Father John's book, *Word Into Silence*, a compendium of his essential teaching, was published. He continued to give the Monday and Tuesday evening talks which the Priory was now beginning to distribute in cassette form under the title, 'The Communitas Series'. He also kept up his correspondence. Rosie Lovat had asked Father John about words like 'empathy' and 'surrender'. He preferred

> empathy more than surrender. Empathy is perfect reciprocity – our dear and courteous Lord invites us to this. Surrender suggests a power of struggle but the essence is pure gift – God gives himself to us and we enter into the fullness of his gift – this is empathy. It puts God and ourselves in a much truer light than surrender – surrender seems to lessen the marvel of his courtesy. . . .
>
> At the end of course it is all words – but some words

reflect the reality a little more clearly – empathy is a bit better than surrender. . . .

I hope I have answered all your questions. Oh yes, there must be no desire for God – rest in him – do not want to possess him. Be still. Desire is not in itself desirable. Desire suggests distance. Jesus tells us that he is with us. More words of course but desire for God is a confusing concept. Realize do not desire.

Then Father John added: 'In the spiritual journey there is neither Greek nor Jew, neither male nor female – only the Lord God and those he loves.' Which was another reason he was so pleased with the first Holy Week services at the Pine Avenue Priory:

On Good Friday for the first time an Anglican Bishop presided at the Liturgy of the Word and the Veneration of the Cross and then I presided at the Liturgy of the Eucharist. We had broken Henry Hill into the Liturgical Function when he helped with the washing of the feet on Maundy Thursday. A very inspiring time.

After Easter Father John made plans for his June trip overseas and wrote to Rosie again, trying to explain one of his favourite distinctions:

About illusions and reality. I think the truth goes something like this. Of course you are right. Reality is everywhere – we have no monopoly of it in Montreal. What I think may be the case, however, is that reality comes in to somewhat sharper focus when you tread the path with the sort of attention we are blessed to enjoy here. It is not only the quiet of the place but the single-mindedness of all those who are here and who come here. Does that sound reasonable?

After his trip to Ireland and a busy summer at the Priory, Father John took a few days in October with the Davitts, at their place on Cape Cod. From there he wrote to Rosie:

I am away in Cotuit on Cape Cod and really enjoying a week of complete change and rest. It is beautiful weather – frosty mornings and bright sunny afternoons with the magnificent Fall foliage brilliant in the sunshine. Yesterday I was on Nantucket Island for the day.

In November Father John wrote to tell Diana of the progress of the Montreal foundation:

> Our work is expanding every week and we are kept busy. Yesterday we had the entire Anglican Hierarchy of four Archbishops and 40 bishops with us for the afternoon. Today we have 14 High School kids from Ontario and the next day a group of Buddhists from Vermont USA!! We are truly catholic.

There is no doubt the Community in Montreal, less than four years old, was thriving on a number of levels. But with the progress and the success there were problems and difficulties. Some of these could be traced to the personality and leadership of John Main himself.

12

The Leader and the Led

Less than a year after arriving in Montreal to establish a new kind of community, John Main confidently wrote to Rosie Lovat: ' . . . we are now coming within sight of our dream – that is a community of monks, sisters, lay community and married people and families – all joined together by meditation. . . .' This was Father John's 'dream' of a new foundation, combining monks and laity in a loving community that would be a witness in contemporary society where communities were disintegrating at every level. He described it for Diana:

> In a previous incarnation I used to worry that people could not see the same vision that I could see – now I only long that they may see some vision. . . .
>
> The danger is that a moment-by-moment life may lack unity and coherence but on the other hand if all you have is vision you may have no moment-by-moment reality.
>
> What I hope for now is that we can live fully in the present moment – fully actualized – fully functioning . . . in full possession of the eternal vision – namely understanding that now is eternity and that eternity is now. Being is all that IS and all that matters.

If we cannot 'be' ourselves, we will never find ourselves in or through others: ' . . . to be is to be yourself. You cannot be for anyone else until you become yourself – actually – really. The most dreadful thing we can do to one another is to try to make the other for me. . . .'

Then the basic teaching, love is impossible without freedom, and freedom is unattainable without detachment:

132

To love is to be in love is to be in the state of detachment. In other words we can only love if we are free to love. The dreadful thing about so much 'love' is that it is possession rather than liberation.

And yet detachment does not sound good to modern ears – or sounds like indifference – which it is not. Can you think of a better word? To be free – to free the other and simply to rejoice together in absolute liberty of spirit. And it is so possible if only we realize it.

There was a final Easter word for Diana who knew what John Main meant by detachment:

Write soon again. It is always a great pleasure to hear from you and share in your movement towards understanding. Everything is devoted to this – to become fully conscious – to be. As Jesus put it, 'I have come that you may have life and have it in all its fullness.'

Easter is the festival of life – risen and limitless.

This was the vision, this was the dream – detachment, freedom, love, fullness of life. A person becoming more real, more oneself, becomes more human. It is possible to realize this growth through a daily commitment to meditation. This was John Main's experience over many years, and it was this experience he had come to Montreal to share with others. The questions must be asked. Why did so few of the original group respond to John Main's vision fully? Why did so many accept his leadership for a time, only to back away later? This was especially true of John Main's fellow Benedictines. Even at Ealing only a few of the monks came to pray at the Meditation Centre. Other than Laurence Freeman no one came from Ealing to join the Montreal foundation. Two American Benedictines did join. Their initial hesitation and their ultimate decision to leave reflect their own concerns about John Main's leadership.

The case of Father Michael Hall is especially revealing. Michael shared John Main's vision of a new monasticism. He planned to join the new monastic community. Then he wrote to Father John in Montreal saying he was having second thoughts and would delay his coming. Father John replied 'that I was very moved by your letter – its honesty – its self-knowledge and its spirit of duty and sacrifice'. He responds to Michael's concerns:

> As to your capacity to live in this sort of community – which is undoubtedly more demanding as it is not easy to escape to the isolation afforded in most monasteries, I am not so sure. I think you would find it much more difficult to live here but I am not at all sure that it might not be the sort of challenge that you need in order to come fully to terms with yourself. But that may sound a little too self-important on my part. I think you have made the right decision for the moment.

He outlines the daily schedule built around three (then four) half-hour meditations a day and including 'Supper followed by recreation – music, etc. (No TV!).' He concludes:

> . . . I really don't think that the 'monastic framework' which you say you may need as support may be as lacking here as you think. Probably because of the smallness of our dilapidated mansion [at this point the community was still at Vendôme] there are more personal demands but I think the round of prayer gives all the support needed if one can commit oneself to it.

But did 'the round of prayer' provide all the support that was needed? For some it did. A young layman named Jaap from Holland lived at the Priory for several months. He came there to pray. While he was there he prayed with commitment. For others 'the round of prayer' was not enough. A Benedictine monk from Ealing planned to spend a few weeks. Within a few days he was so bored he returned home. Other than meditating, preparing meals and washing dishes, what did John Main expect the group would do? In the long term he hoped for a growing community, some of whom would teach meditation, while others would eventually form another foundation.

But in the short term did meditation and, for some, manual work provide sufficient structure? In the ideal world of John Main the nature of one's apostolic work would emerge from the motivation generated in one's prayer life. But this is a gradual process; it takes time. Father John did not have much time. Some younger members of the community – especially those who eventually left – seemed to flounder for lack of direction and content in their day. Even some older Benedictines discovered that, outside the four periods of meditation, the daily regimen was so unstructured as to be insecure. Or was the very simplicity of the structure – prayer, work, reading – so demanding as to be unsettling?

In any event, Michael Hall decided to delay his joining the Montreal foundation. At the same time he advised another Benedictine priest, who consulted him, to consider the Montreal project. Father Paul MacDonald, a teacher in a Benedictine school in Rhode Island, visited the Vendôme Priory. He wrote to Michael Hall that he was favourably impressed with the community and was thinking about 'joining them on an extended basis'. Parts of Paul MacDonald's letter are interesting because of what they reveal about the pros and cons of John Main's leadership, also perceived by others at Ealing and St Anselm's:

> I would like to know what you think about John's foundation – how permanent a move is it in his mind, and do you think he'll stick with it. Obviously no one can predict what the future will bring, especially in a politically uncertain place like Quebec, but I am concerned that it not be a brilliant brainchild of John's which he will tire of in a couple of years.

Paul MacDonald was attracted by the prayer life:

> I am not a prayerful person, not nearly as prayerful as I should be, but that is one of the very things that attracts me about the place – that it would provide a setting for me to grow a lot more in that area. The other thing that I have been screaming about for a long time is community – and the spirit there is just super. I felt it at once and I think it is a rare and precious thing.

Like some other Benedictines, he was concerned about John Main's stability:

> If I were sure about John's long-term complete commit-

ment to it, the recklessness of the thing – the fact that it's small and unestablished – wouldn't bother me at all. . . . The people are delightful, so far as I can see. . . . It is like night and day compared to some of our established houses. . . . And, then, of course, John is a charismatic person in the best sense and I am most attracted to him. Seems to have the discretion that all abbots are supposed to, and yet all the warm, familial qualities that make him a real brother. I hope I'm not too much influenced by the fact that his is such a charming personality – I don't want my going there to be a commitment to one person.

Later Paul MacDonald made another visit to the Vendôme community which he again describes for Michael Hall:

I am seriously considering joining these people . . . I have found the daily routine with the hour-and-a-half of medi- tation, sane and indeed most helpful – but it is quite novel to me, and when I think of persevering in it I really shudder. But I know I could not except in such a setting, in the midst of a group all committed to it. . . . Then, of course, John and Laurence Freeman are a pair of tremen- dously attractive and admirable monks . . . and when all is said and done it is better to be with people one likes on the natural level then with a bunch of people who are struggling to love each other supernaturally because they hate each other naturally. . . . The important thing is that John and the community here are concentrating on basic Xtian monastic and human truths and are undertaking a search which it'd be nice to be a part of. I hope it'll work for me. . . .

When he finally came, things did not work out for Paul MacDonald in the Montreal community. He stayed for several months. Then he left to continue his studies in France with Father John's encouragement and blessing.

There were also problems for the original resident lay community. Five younger people had arrived from England during the first few months the Priory was at Vendôme – although only three or four of them planned to stay indefi- nitely. Pat Hawes, a nurse in her thirties, had first joined

Father John's meditation group at Ealing. Although she always retained her respect and affection for Father John ('He was a good man'), she felt she had been treated badly in Montreal and she was disappointed that the talked-about women's community had not materialized. Father John was not unaware of Pat's discontent and loneliness from time to time in Montreal. He was, in fact, very concerned about her. He was convinced of her serious commitment to prayer and encouraged her to become involved with the meditation groups. But personality problems and other conflicts made a productive life difficult. Pat returned to England and Father John suggested she remain there 'for the moment'. In fact, much to his delight, Pat began work at the Prayer Centre he founded at Ealing, where she continued to help with the meditation groups.

Another early member of the lay community at Vendôme was Nicholas Wardropper, a chartered accountant, then aged 27 who had also lived in the lay community at Ealing and planned to come to Montreal. Father John was pleased to hear from Nicholas that he was coming in the spring of 1978, and replied:

> As you know by now I can't teach you to pray but I can perhaps help you to find a personal discipline within yourself.
>   The basic thing is, as I have always told you, to learn to love. If you come here I hope you will find a group who love you and I hope that you will be able to love us. . . . Here I promise you hard work, frugal living, discipline and a loving concern. . . .

What Nicholas claims to have found at Vendôme was a community run from the top down by Father John and Laurence. He says although there was love in the community there were few external manifestations of it: 'But they were definitely caring. I remember how much Father John and Laurence cared for an elderly neighbour. At its best the Vendôme community was a family.' He considered John Main 'a very funny, very learned, very powerful man'. After about eighteen months Nicholas Wardropper decided he had

137

to make a firm commitment or leave the Montreal community. He left.

Eileen Byrne (who left the Sisters of Sion) also left the lay community later on. She too had known Father John at Ealing, had facilitated his coming to Montreal and helped start the first Christian meditation group in the city. She has vivid memories of Father John:

> I always loved him. I trusted his judgment spiritually. I could feel God's love through him after the meditation. I have not come across anyone else who understands that kind of prayer so deeply. But he had an absolute view of life, of God and of prayer. Other people also have a view of the truth that would be hard for him to accept.

One of the things that Eileen (a painter herself) found hard to accept was a large portrait of Father John by Brenda Bury, who has painted many notable people including Queen Elizabeth the Second. The portrait, hung at the end of a spacious hall, dominates the second floor of the mansion. It is the kind of portrait to which people react in the way Eileen Byrne says people responded to John Main himself: 'People reacted to him violently. Some were outright antagonistic. Some came and left. Others worshipped him. He was larger than life.'

It is not unusual that John Main, like most leaders, aroused strong emotions in other people. Tom Abraham was a bright young man with a doctorate in physics, originally from India. He lived with Father John in the lay community at Ealing, at Vendôme and, for a time, at Pine Avenue. He felt all three to have been happy and productive experiences. He still remarks on Father John's equilibrium: 'I saw him really upset only two or three times in the course of seven years.' Another young man, Paul Lafontaine, remembers coming to supper one evening angry about something or other. After supper Father John called him out to the porch. Paul was afraid he was about to ask him to leave the community for good. Father John said, 'You're obviously upset about something.' Paul blurted out, 'I suppose you want me to leave.' Instead Father John replied. 'It's important for you to be with us – to know even if you are angry we love you very much.' Paul was

stunned: 'He just blew me away. Perhaps I cried. My over-
all impression of Father John was of great gentleness.' Father
John used to say to Brother Laurence and others in the
community: 'Be generous to those who are having a difficult
time and who are not cut out for our life and who will not
stay because later they will look back on a time they were
loved. And it may save them in a moment of despair.'

Lay people seemed to relate better to Father John than did
some Religious and, ironically, this applied especially to other
Benedictines. In 1980 Father Michael Hall resigned the headmastership of St Anselm's School in Washington to come to
Montreal to join the monastic community. At the age of 42
and having discussed at length with Father John the nature
of a new monastic foundation, what did Father Michael
expect when he joined the community:

> I came to Montreal hoping to deepen my prayer life. I also
> hoped to find a meaningful apostolate related to the local
> community. I did not expect to find a democracy but I did
> expect there would be free and open avenues of communi-
> cation. I hoped for a humane and easy relationship among
> the people at the Priory. In a word, I was looking for an
> open community founded on prayer.

What does Michael Hall say he found at the Montreal
Priory? (still at Vendôme when he arrived in the summer of
1980):

> I found a prayer life that was rich and energizing. But I
> also found a kind of direction and governing that, although
> friendly, was patriarchal and very dominant. There were
> no structures that permitted free discussion about the direc-
> tion of the Priory or much of anything else. The governing
> of the Priory was a closed corporation involving Father
> John and Father Laurence and no one else. Seldom did
> anyone else give a talk on meditation. The community in
> residence scarcely did anything together except pray. In
> fact, there was a good deal of talk about community. But
> there was little community in the real sense. Part of the
> problem was that John had no idea what the community
> would do in terms of an apostolate except promote prayer.

He had never thought it through. This uncertainty left a lot of people up in the air.

Others besides Father Michael had raised this question. Was the purpose of the community only to pray? If it had another purpose, what was it? Was the secondary purpose to emerge from the prayer? If so, who would decide and how? There is no doubt that what some perceived as the unfocused nature of the Priory's 'apostolate' caused some uncertainty. In addition there was a certain unavoidable ambiguity in the position of a person like Michael Hall. He was living in the community yet he was not a full-fledged member of it. By the very nature of the foundation (which was not static but developing or, in the words of Father John, 'on the move'), Michael Hall was never completely in nor completely out. His role, unable to be created by a title on a door as in traditional monasteries, would emerge only in time. Gradually Father Michael, somewhat shy and introspective, quietly withdrew from the Pine Avenue community, devoted more attention to his history studies at McGill University in Montreal and after about a year left altogether to resume his academic career in Washington. Some years later Michael, again headmaster of St Anselm's, was comparing notes with Father Paul MacDonald about their experience in Montreal:

> I was astonished at how closely these were in parallel. He too felt that in Montreal he was 'the third man on the bicycle', not really part of the community. When he began to raise questions about the whole thing he was advised to go overseas to mature personally. . . . Like me he retains a respect and affection for John's memory and the realization that to stay in Montreal with the Priory would have been a big mistake.

This is not an unusual pattern for some who came to the Montreal Priory while John Main was leading it – high hopes, disillusionment, departure, often with regret, their respect and affection for John Main himself intact. Did the fact some came and eventually left relate to John Main's own style of leadership and his personality? It is likely. In some respects, John Main was an 'either or', 'all or nothing' kind of leader.

A former colleague at St Anselm's says he was 'unbalanced in the way he went at things', and suggests he was an 'extremist' when it came to matters such as prayer and meditation. Clearly in some matters John Main would not, indeed could not, compromise. If people who came to the Priory remained uncertain about meditation or ambivalent about the mantra, Father John simply restated his teaching. This absolutism extended beyond the spiritual realm. Another Benedictine teaching colleague, Father Aidan Shea recalls:

> John Main's door was always open. But he kept his finger on everything. He wanted to be kept informed. Some people thought he wanted to be kept informed to be sure everything was being done well; others thought he wanted to be kept informed because he wanted to control everything.

Father Aidan liked John Main. He considers he was a 'warm loving, benevolent despot'. John Main's oldest sister, Kitty, is nothing if not direct: 'He was a law unto himself. He was his own person. He made his own decisions.'

It was this decisiveness and despotism, benign though it was, that upset people including some at the Montreal Priory. It translated into small things, a certain rigidity in the schedule, for example, meals hot on the table the moment the noon meditation ended. It also translated into bigger things. Normally consultation in the running of the Priory was not considered necessary, no matter whether you were a former mother superior, a bishop or, indeed, a Benedictine. In some ways John Main ran the Priory the way he baked bread. His Washington friend, Jack Davitt, describes his single-mindedness: 'If he was a guest in your house he had already baked his unique Irish brown bread when you came down to breakfast. "The secret is in the honey," he would say. "That is the *only* way." '

There was only one way to bake bread. There was only one way to squeeze an orange. And usually there was only one way of doing things at the Priory, John Main's way. This does not mean some other way might have worked as well. In fact, considering how few the resources at the beginning and how little the time at the end, John Main's type of leadership may have been the only way. Would anything less than decisive, uncompromising direction have taken a project with almost nothing going for it and transformed it into a viable foundation in less than five years? Would another style of leadership have fulfilled the predictions of most of his critics, that Montreal was a pipe-dream certain to fail? An assessment by John Main's good friend from Trinity, Robert Farrell, may be instructive:

> I would describe Douglas Main/Father John as a masterful man who found the world to be unsatisfactory. Unsatisfactory because it was banal, it was boring and especially because day-to-day existence demanded constant compromise which, try as you might, nibbles away at your integrity.

Any shilly-shallying, any pattern of compromise in the Montreal project would, almost certainly, have destroyed it. John Main was not running in a popularity contest. He was trying to build a foundation from scratch. And like most no-nonsense leaders, he stepped on some toes. What the biographer of the founder of the hospice movement says about the leadership of Dame Cicely Saunders, in some respects, also applies to John Main:

> The pioneering qualities of a founder do not necessarily include the gentle reconciling qualities that make for an easy life as leader ... [Cicely Saunders] finds it easier to relate to people who are content to play second fiddle to her; then she brings out the best in them and rejoices in their success. It is another matter if they challenge her. While she can enjoy anonymity ... she needs to be the leader not the led.

There was never any doubt in Montreal about the leader and the led. John Main was the leader because it was his nature to lead. He was the leader because there was no alternative. Father Laurence Freeman, close to John Main, trusted and trained by him, was not yet thirty. Others who talked about consultation and collegial leadership would have had to challenge John Main, first on the spiritual level, then on the level of sheer physical activity. This none of them were prepared to do and, their ideas of a more traditional community ignored, many of them drifted away.

Still John Main's absolute 'take it or leave it' leadership had its drawbacks. Had he remained absolute in terms of the goal, more flexible in some of the means of achieving it, perhaps more would have stayed. As it was, of the three young men who actually became novices, only one, Paul Geraghty, remained. Only two Benedictines came; neither stayed. The lay community experienced a lot of comings and goings but no steady growth. Would the situation have been different under another kind of leadership than John Main's? Possibly. But the experience of another well-known Benedictine, Bede Griffiths, suggests not. In 1968 he, along with two other monks, joined a foundation (ashram) already in being in the former state of Madras in India. Much later Bede Griffiths wrote to Father Laurence Freeman about the difficulties of establishing and maintaining the kind of community Father John envisaged in Montreal:

> A great deal will depend . . . on whether you can continue to create a genuine contemplation centre where you are. I imagine that by now you have a settled community which has learned to live together for some years. I know from experience how difficult this is. After nearly fifteen years here we are only slowly consolidating our community. Visitors continue to come from all over the world, as I expect they do with you, and stay for weeks or months but the number of permanent members remains small – not more than half a dozen.*

By that criterion, Father John's efforts in Montreal were remarkably successful. Still, it remains true that his style of leadership was not the most appropriate to build a well-knit monastic community; he did not so much form a community as dominate it.

---

* 'Perhaps it is worth mentioning that since 1983 our numbers have shot up to 12 and we are more solidly established than ever. . . . This may be relevant in that it shows how after long and often painful beginnings a community can suddenly "take off".' Bede Griffiths OSB to author, 19 March 1986.

In what way did John Main's personality affect his style of leadership? It did so in a paradoxical manner. In a complex way, John Main, the human being, was the obverse of John Main, the charismatic leader. This was obvious from differing reactions to John Main's leadership at the Priory. The same people who criticized John Main for being autocratic also faulted him for not being sufficiently directive. Those who said John Main dominated other people accused him too of leaving people on their own too much ('high and dry'). In a sense this was true. It reflected John Main's attempt to compensate for what he recognized as a danger in himself, what someone termed 'a streak of authoritarianism'. But this attitude to people went deeper than a matter of compensation, of righting the balance between authority and liberty. Although some perceived John Main as a gregarious extrovert, even a socialite and a monastic dilettante, this perception was far from the truth and sometimes led to misunderstandings. The fact is, John Main, like most of his family, was an extremely private, even shy person. His sister-in-law, Judith Main, noted this: 'the Mains are all deeply private people and none more so than Douglas'.

Integral to his sense of privacy and his natural shyness, was his respect for the other person's liberty and freedom. He would no more invade another person's spiritual space than he would slap a friend on the back. It was not his style. This led to a perception by some that John Main was somehow 'distant' and, in some sense, this also was true. But it must be understood. John Main's 'distance' did not arise from any indifference toward the other person. Rather it was rooted in his respect for the other's integrity – both physical and spiritual. If his 'distance' was seen as mere aloofness, it could easily lead to misunderstandings and even resentments – from being called a 'swell and a toff' to the suggestion he was really only comfortable with the upper-class. Anyone who heard John Main include himself in his 'motley crew' in Montreal could scarcely sustain the view he was a snob. A nun once said she could not stand John Main because of 'his accent'. Others considered 'his accent' and his speaking voice a marvellous instrument to transmit his teaching. His friend, Robert Farrell, remarks:

On the question of Douglas's accent, I think his *natural* accent was a sort of London, classless, educated English, but he had a very good ear and could produce an effortless flow of Irish accented English if the occasion demanded it. If the social circumstances required it he could thicken his accent further and even give it regional inflections i.e. speak in Cork-accented English.

So for some, like Robert Farrell, John Main's 'accent' was an entertaining asset. For others it was just another manifestation of his 'distance'. This was particularly true of those who wanted, or for some reason thought they were entitled to, a special relationship of some kind with John Main. If their attempts to establish one were quietly deflected (or in a few cases rejected) there would be more remarks about John Main's 'distance'. And to this was sometimes added another observation, 'John Main is afraid of intimacy.' This remark was made most often in the matter of his relations with women.

That John Main, a tall, physically handsome man with a compelling speaking voice was attractive to women (and men too) is not surprising. That he was unaware of this attraction (and its dangers) is untrue. In a more general way he was certainly aware of his powerful ability to influence others. It was one more reason he sometimes 'kept his distance'. Often he would use a bit of humour to moderate this influence, for example, tell a joke that fell flat; this only added to the awkwardness and the 'distance'. To say that John Main was afraid of intimacy is too facile. It would be more precise to say that he was wary of intimacy. He knew how magnetic and powerful his personality was. He did not want to take people over or make them over as, in many cases, he could have done. When Paul Lafontaine was spending a lot of time with the lay community at Vendôme he was sometimes a little upset that Father John did not pay more attention to him: ' . . . he was not interested in disciples or in imposing his personality. He was interested in you developing yours. He was aware of teacher-student problems. He was not the guru'.

The other side of this fastidiousness with other people was

that Father John did not want others to possess him. He was, in a sense, a public person, and like many people in the public domain he felt he must defend himself against unreasonable demands and unwanted intimacies. If people made emotional demands or risked inappropriate liberties, he simply tried to distance himself. He did not always do this gracefully. It sometimes happened in a one-on-one situation, where Father John could sometimes be intimidating. Indeed there was an element of awkwardness as there was a streak of authoritarianism in John Main's personality. As a young man this emerged as a long-sleeved gawkiness and an ungainliness in sports. Later John Main tried to smooth out this awkwardness (an element of his shyness) by urbane conversation and Irish charm. Sometimes it worked; sometimes it led to more misunderstanding, a situation that John Main was certainly aware of and that caused him some pain.

It is problematic how much John Main could have done about his natural sense of privacy, his sometimes painful shyness and his awkward relations with some people on a one-to-one basis. But underneath there was something else, something fundamental. It might be described as the solitariness of John Main. He was – under the theatricality, the Irish story-telling, the sophistication and polish, the brilliant achievements – a solitary man. There is a way in which he understood what Thomas Merton meant: 'I can never be anything else than solitary.' This does not mean that John Main, with so many friends, was a lonely man, although some of his closest friends thought, at times, he was. Solitariness however is a deeper notion than loneliness and a more positive one. It implies an ability to stand alone and a free choice to so stand.

Does anyone who knew John Main well doubt he had that ability or that he made that choice? In the beginning he was solitary by nature. Much later, in a paradoxical way, his absolute commitment to love made him a solitary. A meditator in Dublin put it so well: ' . . . he was like someone with a marvellous secret which he had an overpowering urge to share and was just waiting for the right moment to do so; but he kept hoping all the time that you might guess it.' He longed to share but there were not that many to share with.

He hoped that you might guess the secret. Few did. So in a curious way John Main's 'pearl of great price' was also the cause of his solitariness, that, of course, and the absolute nature of his commitment.

John Main's commitment to the goal – freedom to love oneself, others, God – was absolute. But there were those who thought some of his methods were too intransigent, that he demanded too much, that he let people drift when they needed help, that he had a one-track mind when it came to meditation. The man who was closest to Father John during the Montreal period, Father Laurence Freeman, thinks many of these criticisms result from misunderstanding:

> He would take a risk, if the situation required, to induce a person to open up. But he was quick to turn off any hint of infatuation. He wanted a total commitment. The maddening thing was that he would not condemn you even for compromise. He would just remain silent. This silence was more devastating than a reprimand. He was aware of his ability to influence people. His efforts to deal with this, for example, by kidding or joking, led to further misunderstandings.
>
> He did not see himself as just some kind of permission-giver. He made absolute demands on people. He wanted an interior conversion. If they couldn't make it they went away. He used to say 'We don't send them away; they just go.' He saw *crisis* as being a kind of North American institution. He believed in letting people go through a crisis on their own. Normally he thought they would find their own way through meditation.
>
> He was determined not to build a community of people who were emotionally dependent on him. He would sometimes intervene and try to help people at their crisis points. But he did not want to take people over. If people thought something negative about him that was not true, often he did not bother to put it right. He was not afraid of intimacy. He was a person of very pure integrity. Nothing was more painful to him than dishonesty or compromise. He needed clarity in his personal relationships. If he sensed a kind of ambiguity in the relationship he would usually withdraw.

147

Running through Father Laurence's observations, implicit beneath them, is the reality of John Main, the solitary. No words better describe this solitariness – formed in some mysterious way by the tension between John Main, the man, with his human failings, and John Main, the teacher, with the 'secret' he so urgently wants to share – than those of the Irish meditator already quoted, 'the intensity of his presence yet the great depth of his distance'.

Anyone who has examined a painting will have noticed how the shadows emphasize the light. So it was with Father John's leadership. The flaws in his personality served only to light up his strengths as a leader. Whatever difficulties emerged under his leadership in Montreal he never lost the vision from the top of the tower nor, whatever the pressures, compromised it.

But uncompromising leadership and absolute commitment demand a price. Father John hints at the price in these lines to Rosie: 'These have been difficult weeks and your letters are a great encouragement to me. What I am saying is so absolute a commitment that very few can understand it and fewer can commit themselves to it. This is, I suppose, as it should be.' And another time:

'Isn't it funny that a life so simple and so joyful should present so many difficulties for so many people. I sometimes feel as if all the world is going mad! but I suppose the demand of utter simplicity is a great one.'

13

The Teacher and the Teaching

About sixty people of all ages, men and women of several religions and none, wait silently in the meditation room at the Priory on Pine Avenue. Then, quietly, a tall man, straight as a military officer, lightly walks to his chair at the front, gathers his grey-black Benedictine habit about him, sits down and in a compelling, penetrating voice, begins to speak of prayer.

It is unlikely that anyone who came to the Priory to hear Father John talk about prayer (at the weekly instructions or during his homilies at Mass) ever tired of hearing what he had to say. He spoke with an authority and power and confidence that emerged from deep within his personal experience. This confidence did not rely on books of theology. It welled up from the inner resources of a man who had achieved detachment, therefore liberty and therefore love. Those who thought Father John was confident and self-assured were right. But this assurance was a sign of inner conviction, not of arrogance. For whatever one says about John Main's theatricality, whatever the historicity of some of his 'stories', his words, when speaking of prayer, were piercing, authoritative, authentic. There were no false notes. The listeners sensed this. However some related to him personally, there is no doubt he spoke to the meditators in a group with an intimacy that penetrated the heart of each.

By the time he came to Montreal, John Main's expression of his teaching was as transparent as a candle burning in a dark room. Sometimes he would begin with a reference to one of his favourite writers, E. F. Schumacher, author of *Small is Beautiful* and *A Guide for the Perplexed*. He agreed with Schumacher (an economist and more), that our society is

149

confronted with many problems – social, political, educational, economic, religious. Like Schumacher, John Main had concluded the basic problem we all have to face is 'the spiritual problem'. As long as we try to solve our other problems piecemeal, we will never become whole. Or as Schumacher put it: 'People go on clamouring for "solutions" and become angry when they are told that the restoration of society must come from within and cannot come from without.' This clamour for 'quick fixes' and instant answers prescribed from outside by outsiders had long been seen by John Main for what it was, a placebo for a serious disease, part of the problem not the solution because it gave the 'illusion' of something being done.

How could you avoid this illusion and come to grips with the reality of the human condition? In one fashion or another Father John addressed himself to this question in most of his talks on meditation:

> The basic challenge that every human life faces is to come to terms with the essential spiritual reality. That is the underlying phenomenon of what it means to be human. Unless we can come to terms with the basic spiritual being that we are then we will always be dealing with our own life, with relationships, with other people at the surface level. Fritz Schumacher once asked, 'What does it mean to be human?' If we don't grapple with that problem then we will always live at the surface level. Do we want to live as *de facto* materialists throwing a little religion in here and there along the line? Or are we going to live our lives out of the depth of our own capacity to be deeply spiritual men and women? The New Testament summons each of us to live not on the surface or in the shallows but from our own depth of spiritual experience.

This is the way John Main describes the situation of so many modern men and women – hours, days, lives dribbling away, living at a superficial level, living in the shallows. Is that what it means to be human? Will tinkering fix the problem? Or is there a central spine in the person which, if it's not straight, no amount of tinkering – vacations, health clubs, job promotions, another divorce, another marriage – will put it right?

To address these questions John Main cites a man of the sixth century who speaks to our day and our problems: 'St Benedict was able to lead men to organize their lives on a basis that led to depth of spiritual development.' St Benedict asked his followers to organize their daily lives on three bed-rock truths: 'God exists; God revealed himself in Jesus; Jesus sent his Spirit to live in our hearts.' Moreover Benedict required his followers to live these truths, not as theoretical propositions or theological statements but as the DNA of the spiritual life. They are not merely to be pondered; they are to be experienced. How can such truths be experienced? The answer – only through prayer. About 1,400 years ago Benedict sent his followers to John Cassian to learn to pray. Near the end of the twentieth century John Main did likewise.

As his own prayer progressed more deeply on the journey within, John Main's teaching on prayer became more stark and simple. His theology of prayer, related to the bed-rock of Benedict, was crystalline:

> The way for each of us to God is through Jesus. The human consciousness of Jesus in his lifetime gradually became more open to the Father. The extra-ordinary effect of the Redemption is that now, in the glorified life of Jesus, his human consciousness is fully open to the Father. This human consciousness of Jesus is to be found in our own hearts. That's what the In-dwelling of the Holy Spirit means. The supreme task of our life is to open our human consciousness to the human consciousness of Jesus.

The last thing Father John wanted was to complicate his teaching. He stressed its simplicity and clarity (though not its easiness). What then does one make of the words 'open our human consciousness to the human consciousness of Jesus'? Father John himself often said that words and concepts, such as divine love, could only be understood, even partially, by an analogy with the same human phenomenon, in this case, human love. A human lover will open his or her mind and consciousness to the mind of his or her beloved. The two minds and hearts, their values, their feelings for each other

will develop and expand. Some will even say the consciousness of one lover gradually opening to the consciousness of
the other will affect the relationship on the physical level; the
two lovers begin to talk and walk and, in some respects, even
look alike. Or a student opens his mind and consciousness to
that of his teacher. A good teacher will help the student
expand his consciousness. Sometimes close friends will do the
same.

But how can a mere human being open his or her mind to
the human mind of Christ dwelling in the human heart? John
Main's answer, like Benedict's, is in faith, through silence and
prayer. It was his unique contribution that he rediscovered a
way of prayer, refined it and made it relevant for and accessible to contemporary society:

> The essence of the practice of meditation is learning to take
> attention off your self and put it forward, to look out from
> yourself, as it were, to a wider reality so that you're not
> concerned, for example, with any image that you have of
> yourself, but you're only concerned with the reality that is
> there; the reality of which you are a part. The greatest
> hindrance to openness to this reality is that we should
> always be looking into a mirror. If you're always looking
> into a mirror you, first of all, see yourself, and then you
> get only a backwards view of what is there to be seen.

It was John Main's experience that the focus of much
prayer was the 'self', an exercise not of prayer but of intro-
spection and self-analysis:

> For St Benedict each of us should smash that mirror and
> not be looking at that mirror image of ourselves but be
> looking straight forward to creation and to God. The way
> of Benedict is to unhook us from the self-reflective
> consciousness so that when we sit down to pray we're not
> praying about ourselves. If you keep asking God to do
> things for you, your time of prayer is one prolonged ego
> trip. You become more deeply hooked into yourself.
> Benedict taught that to gain freedom of spirit you must be
> un-hooked from your own self-conscious pre-occupations.

152

Benedict saw that we must direct our gaze to wider creation – the love of God as revealed in Jesus.

Although he cites Benedict, John Main is addressing the problems of our own day:

> Everywhere I travel, in North America, Europe, Australia, the East, I find people are searching for a way back to their own true selves. They are searching for a way forward to harmony – with their own spirit, with their neighbour, with God. Self-analysis won't do it. We've been analyzed to death. Our society is seeking a way out of the labyrinth of self-consciousness. Our contemporaries are not seeking a way of evasion nor a way of oblivion. They are seeking a way of full consciousness and real integrity. They are looking for a place in which they can come to this full consciousness.

For Father John that place was through meditation. Why did he have so powerful an attraction to people, many of them young people? Why is it that the prayer he taught has such surprising appeal for the middle-class, especially the managerial group whose careers are so directed at the top and whose lives are often so fragmented at their base? The reason is not just his teaching on meditation. It is also the clarity with which he described and diagnosed so much of our contemporary condition – half lives lived at half throttle by people who are half there:

> Each of us must accept our responsibility to be fully alive at this present moment – to be the person we are called to be. The anxiety, the alienation and the boredom with which so many people today are afflicted is the result of this failure to be fully human, to be fully alive. So many people respond to this ennui by trying to possess or control life. But the call of Jesus is if you would find your life you must be prepared to lose it. It is in prayer that we lose our life totally. We lay aside our own thoughts, our own ideas, our own imagination. In the silence and simplicity of meditation we are as open as we can be in this life to the life of Jesus.

This way of prayer was not a lonely, individual way. For Father John it was a way of union that led naturally to community. The task of Christian meditation is to leave self behind and to go forward into the mystery of God. But turning toward God in meditation was also turning toward others in God. This mysterious union, in faith, with God in prayer is one that must be shared. It must be shared, even proclaimed, not as some solitary experience, but in the same way as the good news of the Gospel should be shared and proclaimed. So Christian meditation, by its very nature, leads to community. It requires community, the way a child needs friends.

That is why Father John encouraged meditators to form small groups to pray together, perhaps once a week in their homes or some other appropriate place. He called these groups, of which he was very fond, 'communities of faith'. It is part of his vision that Father John saw the Church, including its structures, being transformed by these 'communities of faith' committed to the contemplative experience:

> Perhaps the greatest challenge facing Christian people today is to find themselves communities of faith where we leave the world of materialism and enter the greater reality and learn to see the material world interpenetrated with the love of God. . . . If we can find small groups who are becoming who they are called to be by Jesus Christ they will have power and authority and love. Rather than seeking to convert others we will be living our own conversion and creating a vortex of love and will lead others into the same experience.

He once wrote: 'We have known both liturgical renewal and biblical renewal. It is absolutely necessary that we have a true experience of God and know renewal in prayer.' But how could this be effected? 'Nothing could be simpler,' said Father John, 'than to open our hearts to the divine Indwelling.' 'But nothing', he said, 'demands more faith – that is the challenge.'

This was the challenge – love through freedom – and this was the way – meditation and the mantra – that Father John constantly placed before his listeners. So careful himself about the use of the precise word, he was well aware of the problems of language when it came to describing any religious process. That was why he insisted on returning to the importance of silence. His own experience was that silent meditation, prayer without words, thoughts or images, was an experience that renewed other religious practices and made them fresh. For example, Father John remarked on the need for the Church to get back to the devotion to the Sacred Heart, 'devotion to the love of Jesus as the revelation of the love of the Father'.

Never did he imply that meditation was a flight from reality nor could he understand those who did. He once put this view to Diana in a graphic way:

Are there not, broadly speaking, two types of persons? The person who looks out on the chaos that is reality and shrinks back in fear. In order that living is possible this person creates the neat and ordered society or garden or backwater where all the lines are straight and everything is under control and predictable. It is of course all illusion and flight from reality. The other person is the one who looks the chaos in the eye and recognizes that he or she is not only part of the chaos but that the chaos is right inside his or her own head and heart.

Living with this reality one tries to understand the dynamic that is at work in the chaos and to see *its* ordered place if one can only see the balance behind all the wild explosions of life. What we have to do is not so much to *tame* as to understand with sympathy, empathy and compassion the reality that is outside of us and the *reality* that is within us.

As an experienced teacher, widely read in the theology of prayer, Father John was aware of the concerns that Christian meditation raised for some people. Although he treated their concerns seriously his answers were usually pragmatic, related to his own experience in prayer rather than to theories about it. To paraphrase the author of *The Imitation of Christ*, Father John thought it more important to experience prayer than to be able to define it. Still, the questions would come, sometimes after a talk on meditation. Was this the only way to pray? No, but the only way Father John had found that

155

worked for him. Did Christian meditation conflict with other personal and liturgical prayers? If anything it enhanced and enriched them. Meditators who read the Scriptures or said the Office remarked how meditation gave a new depth and freshness to both.

A more serious objection described Christian meditation as another form of an old aberration, Quietism, consisting of a kind of passive devotional contemplation, the powers of the will suspended and the senses ignored. Father John's response to the problem of Quietism was usually placed in the context of a double deformation in much contemporary prayer. The first is the attempt 'to reduce God and his infinity within the limitations of our finite minds'. Of the temptation to reduce God to our level Father John says: 'Meditation is so important because it leads us beyond the images and concepts that we can so easily use to try to control the divine presence. It leads us indeed beyond all egotistic "desire" for God.'

The opposite of this attempt to bring God down to our level is the temptation to be passive and inactive, to construct a soft mental mattress on which we 'rest' in God or 'dream' of him. Father John calls this

> the danger to the modern mind of a new sort of quietism – a new sort of passive sentimentality. Prayer, above all else, is not a nostalgia for God. Prayer is the summons to a full experience of the living Christ whose purpose, as St Paul telis us, 'is everywhere at work'. St Paul's emphasis is not on religion as anaesthesia – thinking about an absent God and absenting ourselves from the present moment to be lost in a kind of pietistic dalliance. . . . The call of prayer, in short, is to be fully alive in the present, without regret for the past or fear of the future.

In both his talks and his writings Father John rejected the notion that modern Quietism, 'passive sentimentality' was in any way characteristic of Christian meditation: ' . . . meditation has nothing to do with quiet reverie. It has to do with wakefulness. We awaken to our nearness to God.' Or: 'There is nothing passive whatsoever about meditation. It is a state of growing and deepening openness. . . .' It is not nostalgia for God.

The suggestion that Christian meditation is a version of modern-day Quietism (a lazy forty-winks in the divine 'presence') has emerged because of two problems. Father John referred to the first in his Wimbledon retreat. 'Some religious people like being slightly stoned in a religious way.' The religious person is then in a 'half-living limbo'. It is easy to become stranded in this 'lazy hazy' spirituality and make no further advance. The second problem is a misconception of the role of the mantra. The mantra, Father John taught repeatedly, must be said continually from the beginning of the meditation to the end. It must be said silently, interiorly, mentally, at a steady pace (somewhat like the metronome on a piano) without stopping. What if the meditators become aware that they are not saying the mantra? Then they should begin saying it again as gently and as quickly as possible.

Why this insistence on the continual mantra? Simply because the mantra is not a technique to achieve a goal, e.g. inner peace or a sense of 'presence'; it is a discipline to turn the meditator away from self and to dispose the meditator, in silence and faith, for the action of God. The action of God, of the Holy Spirit, normally occurs at the deeper subconscious levels of the human being. If the purpose of the mantra were to achieve inner serenity, tranquillity, a sense of 'presence' then, of course, it would make sense to stop saying the mantra when the 'presence' is achieved and to start saying the mantra when the 'presence' vanishes. This is something else, the 'stop and go' mantra, sometimes referred to as the 'intermittent' mantra. At best it is a technique that alters one's psychic state. At worst it appears to be an attempt to manipulate the Holy Spirit. This is not to say that the 'presence' in which one rests is not a good thing. It often results in a sense of refreshment and improved health also found in Transcendental Meditation. As the Boston writer and philosopher, Andrew Foley, has observed, the 'intermittent mantra' does not involve the meditator with the divine presence but only with another (albeit deeper) aspect of the human psyche.

Father John also comments on this confusion in terms of one of the aims of the 'intermittent' mantra, i.e. to uncover the person's 'centre' where God is present:

... it seems inadequate to say this is just 'centring ourselves' or even 'finding our centre'. We do this too, but not if it is our conscious aim – that would be too self-conscious, too desiring. We find our centre only by placing ourselves in the silence of God beyond any image or centre or circumference. What we think of as 'our' centre is too often an illusion of the self-reflecting ego, somewhere we like to take up our stand and observe God at work in us. But this can never be the way.

As for the technique of the 'intermittent' mantra, Father John sees it as another item of our disposable society:

Any technique of prayer is by definition impatient. It sets out to make things happen according to the desire we have for God, to possess God – a desire that operates within the limitations of our sense of time. It will, then, be a disposable method, used until it produces a desired effect, then dropped and taken up again when we want more.

Father Laurence Freeman also made a distinction between the mantra as 'technique' (controlling) and the mantra as 'discipline' (disposing):

... to experiment with meditation is to devalue it to the status of a tool or technique at the service of our desire to possess or control. The utterly simple teaching of saying the mantra from the beginning to the end of each meditation is peculiarly vulnerable to such distortion. But if we do not intend to say it continuously we are making it a tool. If on the other hand we learn to begin, to persevere – this may take us some time – then we are transcending *technique* and egoism in the faithful practice of a discipline.

Reduced to its simplest terms, the primary aim of the continual mantra is to keep saying it continually and, if possible, to listen to its being said. That is all. The secondary aim is to take one's mind off oneself and to dispose oneself for God's action which (as Andrew Foley observes) occurs at the divine (and normally subconscious) level over which the meditator has no control or even awareness. It would be as futile for a meditator to try to influence God's action using the technique of the 'intermittent' mantra as it would be for an impatient motorist to attempt to change the colour of a traffic light by blowing his horn.

This does not mean that saying the mantra continually (for the half-hour period) cannot have an unusual effect on the purely natural level. It can and it sometimes does. Father John describes how the meditator, at the beginning of the pilgrimage, 'must confront with some shame the chaotic din of a mind ravaged by so much exposure to trivia and distraction'. Elsewhere he compares the chaos of the mind to a tree filled with chattering monkeys:

> Persevering through this in fidelity to the mantra, we then encounter a darker level of consciousness, of repressed fears and anxieties. The radical simplicity of the mantra clears this too. But our first inclination is always to retreat from the dawn of self-knowledge. . . .
>
> In entering upon these first two levels, of surface distractions and subconscious anxiety, we risk being bruised.

Father John also compares this possible phenomenon in meditation to

> breaking through the sound barrier. When you come to that point there can be a lot of turbulence. It is at this moment that the discipline you have learned by saying your mantra and by faithfully continuing to say it, will enable you to be entirely open to the love of Jesus which takes you through it.

What he refers to here is the 'turbulence' sometimes stirred up when the mantra, resonating like a tuning fork between the conscious and subconscious psyche, to some degree opens the conscious to the subconscious. This permits material from the subconscious, some of it healing, some of it painful, to flow into the conscious mind. It is the painful material (e.g. subconscious memories) that can sometimes provoke 'turbulence'. But, ultimately, the whole process is a healing, unifying one, bringing all levels of consciousness into harmony. The action of God, grace, builds on nature, preferably a whole and healthy nature. At the natural level Christian meditation helps to unify our split and divided pysche. This is not its primary function but it is a lateral benefit that continues at the subconscious level and disposes the meditator, growing more unified and whole, for the work of God at the deeper, silent levels. ·

Another objection to Christian meditation, is that it is 'non-incarnational' because it dispenses with discursive reasoning, a hallmark of Ignatian spirituality:

> The most frequently heard objection to meditation – one that often came from Religious – was that it was 'one-sided', concentrating on our spiritual side to such a degree that it rejected our reason and imagination and so could not be truly called incarnational.

Father John did not deny there could be a legitimate debate about some modalities of the theology of prayer. But he felt the debate was ultimately sterile unless it ultimately led to praying. He felt this type of objection

> . . . could only be made before the experience of meditation has been entered into: the experience of the integration of mind and heart [the whole psyche] in a silence beyond the limitations of the self-reflective consciousness. The experience of this integration pervades the whole mystery of the meditator's life.

Those people who have been struggling for a lifetime with discursive prayer buttressed with booster-shots from the imagination will appreciate what Father John is talking about. But what, the objection recurs from those brought up on the flights of fancy of Archbishop Alban Goodier, does this approach mean for the 'historical Jesus'? It means, from the perspective of Christian meditation, focused on the eternal 'now', the present moment of the Risen Christ, that the historical Jesus becomes more 'real' and less a 'fantasy', an illusion of the imagination.

A final question, often directed at Father John after his talks,was about distraction in meditation. After encouraging his listeners to ignore distractions as much as possible, he usually said that Christian meditation was the ideal prayer to deal with distractions:

It is the way *par excellence* to handle distractions because the purpose of the one word is simply to bring your mind to peace. Not to bring it to rest with holy thoughts alone but to transcend what we know as thoughts altogether. And the mantra, serving this end, is like a plough that goes through your mind pushing everything else aside – 'making the rough places plain'.

Then he reminded his listeners of John Cassian's view of the mantra and distractions:

You remember what Cassian said of its 'casting off and rejecting the rich and ample matter of all manner of thoughts'. It is because the mind is 'light and wandering', as susceptible to thoughts and images as a feather to the slightest breeze, that Cassian enjoins the mantra as the way to transcend distraction and attain stability.

Father John never claimed that saying the mantra continually for twenty minutes to half an hour twice a day would eliminate distractions much less work any miracles. A woman at a meditation talk once asked him about 'visions'. 'Madame,' he replied, 'if you have any, return to saying your mantra as quickly as possible.' Nothing 'happens' during meditation and if it does, treat it as suspect. What Father John did claim was that daily faithfulness to meditation, being on the way, 'on the pilgrimage' as he often called it, would gradually effect a change in a person's attitudes and values. Father John refers to this in *The Gethsemani Talks:*

The universal testimony of our prayer groups is that when they have been meditating for a period of six months or so they begin to look at their lives by a different set of values. They all say they find the quality of their life is itself beginning to change.

Imperceptibly, priorities begin to change. In a paradoxical way, the spiritual part of life becomes a little more 'real', and the material part a little more 'illusory', a little less important. There is more freedom because there is more detachment. There is more love because there is more freedom. None of the changes are sudden. But they are essential if one is seriously to address the question: 'What does it mean to live a human life? How does one become more "fully alive"?' For some it means, for the first time, that the choices they make are made freely. The essential direction of their lives emerges from within; it is not dictated from without. To some this might seem like a small change, in fact, it is a radical one. Other people usually notice the change before the meditator does. And usually the meditator notices a change not during the meditations themselves, but long afterwards when decisions are made about priorities, work, people, that have never been made before.

A missionary priest from Africa, Father John Smith, first heard about Father John on the cassettes he had made to explain meditation:

> I was desperately searching for something in my prayer. I was faithful to daily meditation but very dissatisfied.
>
> The breakthrough came when I listened to Father John. I felt called TO LET GO, TO MAKE THE JOURNEY WITHIN, TO BE IN SILENCE and simply trust. That's what I needed to hear.
>
> It was his *authority* that appealed to me – he spoke from the *heart* – from what he himself was experiencing. I could tell that in his voice although I never met him. Then his *simplicity* spoke loud and clear. Along with that was his *vision* that set me on the road I was searching for. It was because he knew where he was going, where meditation would lead, that he could be so convincing.

Some time later Father Smith met Father John for the first time at the Priory on Pine Avenue as he joined the community for their Holy Week retreat:

> I experienced him as the Guru – the man who didn't direct retreats (as I had expected) but who simply said: 'Meditate with me.'
>
> When I was leaving to return to the missions I shared my concern that it was easy to be faithful to meditation in the monastery but what about the busy life of the missionary? He simply said: 'What alternative have you'?. . .

As a missionary I feel the need for this 'depth living'. Instead of action now it is being and I find this far more fruitful and life-giving in every respect. It's really a paradox. But I know from living this way of life how much more missionary I am . . . I owe this conviction to Fr John.

Others were now hearing of Father John for the first time through his writings. This was the reaction of a professional woman:

I first learned of him in September 1981 when I was feeling a need to deepen my spiritual life and came across *Talks on Meditation* in a book store . . . I immediately started using the method of the mantra and then made arrangements to spend the New Year's week-end at the monastery together with my husband who had been practising meditation although not with a mantra. We were both very impressed with Father Main and each of us had a couple of talks with him. What impressed us was his 'with-it-ness' (if there is such a word) – that is when he spoke to a person, he was intent, listening and wholly there. He practised what he was preaching in meditation.

Occasionally Father John would write a word of encouragement: 'Meditation changes our life and we all need great encouragement as we face the new dimension.' Paul Lafontaine, after he began to meditate regularly with the community at Vendôme, wrote:

Meeting Father John and becoming his friend . . . was a great gift for me. I have often had the strong feeling since, that he called me specially to the work of meditation: to go beyond my worthlessness into an infinite expansion of spirit. Although he was a man of big notions, great gestures, refined tastes, and a deep understanding of ritual, by far my most pervading thought of Father John is of a man who was very gentle. A man who saw into my heart and uncovered my anger.

The influence of Christian meditation was growing. While Father John was teaching meditation in Montreal, the revolution was emerging in Iran. One of those caught in the

pre-revolutionary violence was the Bishop of the Episcopal
Church in Iran, the Right Reverend H. B. Dehqani-Tafti. He
narrowly escaped assassination, his wife was wounded, his
only son was murdered. The Bishop writes in his book about
the Iranian Revolution, *The Hard Awakening*:

> Christians receive from God the power to carry out their
> mission in life. They get this power through prayer. I have
> always found prayer difficult, but I have never given it up
> completely. My main difficulty has always been lack of
> concentration. . . .

Then the Bishop describes how John Main entered his life:

> I greatly benefited, about a year before the revolution, from
> a course of twelve tape-recorded talks on meditation. . . .
> They had been prepared by John Main, a Benedictine
> father. . . . The basis of the technique is to sit in silence
> twice a day, each time for not less than twenty minutes,
> repeating to oneself a short phrase from the Bible. Though
> I found this simplified the problem of concentration, it did
> not make it easier; indeed real simplicity is always difficult
> to achieve. But at least I learned where I was; and I
> continued to persevere, sitting in solitude, and repeating
> what Father Main calls a 'mantra', a word borrowed from
> Indian religious tradition.

The Bishop did not think he had come upon Christian meditation by accident:

> I now believe that God was teaching me this method of
> meditation to help me to face the oncoming storm. One of
> the things it did was to bring me face to face with myself.
> It worked like a vacuum-cleaner, drawing out of my inner
> being everything that was consciously untrue. More and
> more, I came to realize . . . unless you are true to yourself,
> you cannot face difficulties and suffering creatively.

If the clarity of his message and its profound, though gentle
effect on many who heard it, characterized Father John's
teaching, there were other influences in his life that gave his
message its colour and texture. One was his beloved Ireland
with its green hills (tramped so often with his cousin, Father

Paddy Crean), and above all, the Irish people grounded in a faith all the more unshakeable because it was so ancient. In his later years he seldom spoke about the anguish in Ireland. John Main's silence was revealing. He could not bear to speak of 'the troubles' that had so ravaged the country he loved.

Father John's love of Ireland was, in a sense, a facet of his love for the Church. But, as with his country, he was not blind to the problems of the institutional Church. Nor was he afraid to criticize church authorities, even when a Pope as popular as John Paul II, preaching so much about human rights, was seemingly ignoring the rights of priests and nuns. John Main wrote to Rosie Lovat: 'We are a bit disappointed with the Pope. It seems too much like a circus – too much talk about human rights and too little evidence of an awareness of the tragedy of lonely priests and nuns trying to get to a better life.'

To the renewal of the Church in the modern world, Father John linked the refurbishing of Mary, the Mother of God. In terms of meditation, he saw Mary as the great exemplar of other-centredness; 'She is the greatest human example of interiority; she kept all these things in her heart.' Once when Diana wrote to question Mary's relevance for the contemporary woman, Father John replied:

> To turn to your point on Mary the Model of Prayer. I don't think she is just the model for obedient women! As far as I can tell she was a very courageous woman – stayed by the boy when everybody else beat it – but I think she is a valuable model for us all in her practice of silence – her steadfastness and her full acceptance of her own destiny. In other words my feeling is that she doesn't display submissive female characteristics but fully human responsiveness to her life – which is what one would hope all women and all men do.

There was a final influence on John Main, allied to Mary, his own mother, Eileen. She had a deep but natural faith, natural in the sense it was spontaneous and joyous and integrated into her daily life. It was this faith, serious but not solemn, that John Main inherited from his mother.

Father John once said, 'It is not possible to teach prayer

if a person does not practise it himself.' So it was one of the
joys of his almost yearly trips to Ireland (besides the short
visits with his mother and the family) that he had the opportunity to teach prayer to many of his own people and to pray
with them. A meditator in Dublin remembers the impact his
teaching made on her:

> I don't know whether or not it was because of his spectacles
> but his eyes seemed particularly brilliant as he told us what
> would happen if we persevered in our meditation – 'it is
> like looking through a glass which at first is a bit unclear,
> then you polish it and it becomes a little clearer, and you
> keep polishing it, and gradually it becomes clearer and
> clearer' – then he was still for a minute before he added –
> 'and sometimes there isn't any glass there at all'. I have
> never forgotten those words of Fr John and the meaning
> he gave to them as he spoke.

Once having heard John Main, the teacher, it would be
difficult to forget his words. His aim was not to direct others
but that they should find their own direction. He did not
pressure people, even those who misunderstood his teaching.
As the meditator in Dublin said: 'This was the amazing thing
about Fr John, no matter how much he had to teach or
correct or answer silly questions he never hurt anyone because
of the love and joyfulness with which he reached out to us.'

Others seemed to have been waiting for his teaching on
prayer all their lives. As the woman manager of an art gallery
in Boston explained: 'He got it right, you know, he got it
right. He believed in you, saw what you could be. I had the
feeling that after all these years I might just get it together.'
There was still much Father John had to teach, many others
to whom he would reach out in love and joyfulness. But there
was not much time. Only a little more than a year.

14

The End of the Beginning

Sometimes John Main perplexed others, even members of his own family when they noticed he scarcely ever wanted them to see him off on a journey. Usually he preferred to go to the airport or the train station alone. His older sister, Yvonne, surmised that he found partings of that kind too difficult. Father John once touched on 'partings' with Diana:

> Do you know it struck me the other day that the mystery of life is closed to us until we realize that life is in essence a tragedy – in no morbid sense – but in the sense of facing reality. What it is all about more than anything else is – parting. We are always parting – sometimes temporarily, sometimes permanently. I think that when we can face this we can for the first time understand how important it is to love and cherish one another before the parting – indeed all relationships are ultimately a preparation for the parting – just as our own lives are a preparation for our own deaths.
>
> This may sound all rather morbid but I think if you can follow my tortuous reasoning you will see what I really mean is that once you understand the tragedy then you will prepare for the parting by the most amazing love and cherishment so that the parting is indeed such sweet sorrow.

Those lines of bitter-sweet sorrow, so real, so Irish, were also prophetic. For Father John and for all those he loved and cherished the time of permanent parting was approaching. At the beginning of 1982 Father John was scheduled to visit the meditation groups in Africa. Instead Father Laurence went in his place. One of the reasons was a nagging midwinter cold that seemed to sap his energy. He spoke casually about

167

this to his regular physician, Dr Arthur Nancekivell. The doctor prescribed a cold remedy that eased the problem.

But in February the cold recurred. And this time there was a complication. When he lay down to rest Father John experienced some difficulty in breathing accompanied by a wheezing sound. In early March he contacted Dr Nancekivell again. This time, the doctor, somewhat concerned because of Father John's past medical history with cancer, suggested he come into the Queen Elizabeth Hospital for an examination. Father John did so on 10 March. Tests and X-rays were taken. These included a biopsy of lung tissue. The verdict was devastating. There had been a spread, a metastasis, of the primary cancer in the bowel to Father John's lungs. Multiple cancerous nodules were growing on both lungs. The doctors now knew that minute cancer cells, present before the previous operation in October 1979 (and undetectable by medical science), had spread from the original site and, over the intervening years, had 'seeded' the lung area. The result was advanced secondary cancer in the lungs. One of the cancerous nodules, pressing on an air-flow to the lungs, was causing the wheezing Father John had experienced.

Dr Nancekivell, not just Father John's doctor but his friend, immediately called an oncologist, a specialist in cancer, Dr Joan Zidulka. Dr Zidulka knew from her medical experience that in a case such as this there was little or no evidence 'that any treatments would either prolong life or improve the quality of life'. Dr Nancekivell concluded that the medical situation was 'hopeless'. He said as much to Father John: 'He told me then he thought he might be able to beat it. And from that time on I never saw him manifest the slightest evidence of depression or ultimate fear.' Dr Zidulka also makes the point that while at that time Father John's medical condition was terminal 'he was not dying'. Neither the doctors nor Father John knew how much time was left but then, in March, none of them thought it would be so short.

The doctors went to work immediately to do whatever medicine could to alleviate the situation. Radio-therapy treatments were begun to reduce the cancerous nodules in his lungs. He responded well to the treatment and the breathing problem was eliminated. To contain the spread of the cancer,

Dr Zidulka ordered a series of chemotherapy treatments. Consideration was given to sending Father John for examination elsewhere. The doctors made inquiries at the best medical centres in the United States, such as the Sloan-Kettering in New York and the Mayo Clinic in Minnesota. But the response from these prestigious institutions was unanimous. No effective treatment had been discovered to cope with the spread of cancer from the colon. Dr Zidulka decided that nothing would be gained by sending Father John away from his home in Montreal.

In fact, with the breathing situation cleared up and his cold gone, by the beginning of May Father John was feeling much better. At first no one except Father John himself, his doctors, and those he told (Father Laurence and Rosie Lovat) knew how serious his medical situation was. It was decided to keep the matter confidential and to carry on as normally as possible. He continued his twice-weekly talks to meditators (to whom he seemed his usual robust self) with no perceptible loss of vigour, clarity or sense of humour. He had maintained his heavy correspondence from the time he had begun to feel unwell. To a Canadian meditator concerned about the role of confession in the Church, he related confession to one of his seminal beliefs, the influence of the cosmic Christ:

> Confession . . . is above all a recognition in faith of the presence of Jesus in our midst – it is a recognition that we are part of his Body and if we fail him we go to him in his Body to externally confess our sin and to receive our pardon for the external consequences of our sin.

This observation on confession in the Church is revealing for what it says about Father John's view of theology. Radical as he was in his teaching on prayer, radical in the sense of returning to roots, he was, in many respects, a conservative in theology. Father John's perception of the cosmic Christ, like that of the Jesuit scientist, Father Teilhard de Chardin, was of a Christ who had a relevance for all creation. And this universal view came through in his talks. A young Montreal meditator and mother, Polly Scofield, says:

That was what was so wonderful about him. He had a

vision of the universal Christ who dies once and for all for the whole of humanity – not just for a little 'itty bitty' narrow group of Christians. I just remember when someone said it is the Cross of Christ that saves us, he said, 'No, it is the love of Christ.'

In the spring too he polished the 'Introduction' to *Letters from the Heart* and the book was published. On Good Friday he participated in a programme on the Canadian Broadcasting Corporation exploring spirituality. Early in June the Abbot-General of the Benedictines in Rome came to Montreal to visit the Priory. Of course, during this period, Father John was in close contact with his doctors. He had responded well to the radio-therapy treatments (although he was laid low for a few days by a severe back pain in mid-May). By the end of May he was looking well, feeling fine and preparing for a trip to Ireland. He went to the Queen Elizabeth Hospital for a chest X-ray on 28 May. Despite the external signs of health, the X-ray showed the cancer in Father John's lungs had become much worse. That did not change his plans about Ireland. Dr Joan Zidulka noticed how determined he was to go despite the ominous results of the X-ray: 'He was not upset or angry. He was not hostile to the doctors as some cancer patients are. He struck me as a man who knew what was going to happen and wanted to live life to the full. I think that explains the Irish trip.'

What also explains the Irish trip was Father John's desire to be with the meditators of his own country and the members of his family one last time. (Although, as he had told one of his doctors, Father John was still hopeful he could defeat the disease). Despite the physical demands, he gave retreats and talks on meditation in London, Liverpool, Manchester, Kylemore and Dublin. It was to be his last visit to the places and the faces that had shaped his life through the years. Friends perceived no physical problem (except occasionally a slight limp when he was overtired) and he did not discuss it. His family, particularly his sisters, Yvonne and Diane, noticed only that at times he seemed slightly preoccupied. When they went on a drive half way across Ireland, instead of chatting animatedly as usual, Father John said he preferred to listen to music. One of the meditators in Dublin did notice a change:

> I must say . . . that I noticed a great difference in Dom John during his 1982 visit to us. There seemed to be a certain brilliance about him, not only in mood but in aura. He was in excellent spirits, very available to everybody and radiating an intense dynamism of affection.

Indeed, considering his physical condition, it was remarkable how available Father John was on this final trip. It was as though he feared he might miss someone. One night he spoke about meditation to a large crowd in the lovely convent chapel in Glenmaroon. In the question period a meditator asked whether 'It would be a good idea to match the saying of the mantra to one's breathing'. Father John replied, 'It doesn't really matter whether one does or not, but please do keep breathing at all costs.' After the meeting, more tea and chatting. Father John left about 10.45. But the schedule for the next day, as recorded by the Dublin meditator, was heavier than ever:

> Wednesday was our big day, a happy family day, a feast day. Fr John arrived at 11 o'clock and we started the day with a talk about meditation for any newcomers. No matter how many talks on meditation I had heard, each one seemed new and necessary! In this one Fr John said that he could sum everything up into just three words – 'SAY YOUR MANTRA', a simple, straightforward message. . . .
>
> We lunched at 1 o'clock and from then until 3.30 Fr John remained in one of the parlours for anyone who wished to have a private word with him. A queue formed at once. . . . There was another quick cup of tea then, and even here Fr John was besieged with people.

Usually when Father John went to Ireland he was so 'besieged with people' that he had too little time for his own family. His eldest sister, Kitty, could not understand this (or meditation either) and it often made her cross. His new sister-in-law, Judith, married to Father John's handsome and debonair brother, Ian, had a different view. She met Father John for only the second time during his visit in the summer of 1982. But Judith, an attractive and perceptive woman, had long been both puzzled and intrigued by what she had heard about John before she met him:

> . . . it seemed to me that there were two different men in question. The first was the deeply spiritual individual of the tapes and the booklet whose teaching struck deep chords in me, especially with regard to the simplicity of his message. . . .

Father John's simple message was one influence that led Judith to become a Roman Catholic:

> The thought that here was a Catholic priest who could see through all the 'worldly' aspects of the tradition of the Church back to the essential spirit of the teaching of Our Lord made me feel that here at last was where I 'belonged'.

But long before that happened, Judith had heard a lot about the 'other' John Main:

> The second man was the individual his family talked about – with great affection, but always rather tongue-in-cheek as if one shouldn't take him too seriously. The feeling was that he was always doing extraordinary things and pulling people's legs – he was a great practical joker. The traditionalists, in religious terms, of the family were plainly shocked by his apparently unorthodox approach to his chosen vocation of monk. There were half-serious references to his 'going monking'; his new 'religion'; his grey habit; the magnificent house presented to the community in Montreal, etc. ('What price the vow of poverty, etc?') He naturally attracted, and was attracted to, the influential and the wealthy . . . but the family was inclined to wonder whether he was being 'affected'. At first I was rather shocked by these references. It seemed to me quite inconceivable that the man who had made the tapes could possibly be the semi-charlatan which was almost what was implied. . . .

That was Judith's rather confused image of Father John (Douglas) until she met him for the first time in 1980:

> I finally met Douglas in the bosom of his family in Dublin,

and for two days saw his rather austere figure (with a twinkle in his eye) thaw out more and more under the familiar teasing and become once more the much-loved rogue – the younger brother who loved to play a practical joke. As the newest member of the family I was fair game, of course, and being impressed as I was to meet this extraordinary man, it threw me a little at first to have remarks made to me with the greatest gravity and all the authority of the great teacher, only to find that I was having my leg pulled unmercifully!

Judith then remarks what everyone noticed, how close Father John was to his family:

The importance of the family in his life was exceptional. . . . The Mains are unusually close, with deep ties of affection (not shown directly, but clearly understood) which are usually expressed in joking terms . . . I think that to have become a monk and, to a great extent, to have cut himself off from his family must have been a far harder deprivation than any other for him.

It was in June during his last visit to London that Judith Main met Father John again:

The second time I met him was in 1982 in London to give a retreat, which we attended, in Neasden. It was a perfect day of peace and joy and deeply serious purpose and the first time I had seen him as 'teacher'. I will never forget the deep conviction and sincerity of what he said and the look of radiant integrity on his face. No one could imagine for a second that he was not in total earnest and speaking from personal experience. The atmosphere of that day, pervaded by his personality, will always remain one of the few glorious occasions of my life (another was the day of his Memorial Mass when he was most tangibly 'present' and transformed a tragic occasion into one of pure joy).

Finally, Judith Main tried her hand at reconciling the two John Mains – the spiritual rogue – a task that baffled most of those who knew him:

I think an important clue to his character is that he would

(probably) not have liked me to write this. Under all their easy, teasing charm the Mains are all deeply private people and none more so than Douglas, who had large areas of his life about which no one knew anything in the family. I think this is the reason for the apparent dichotomy in his character and, of course, also for his extraordinary success in being both a man of the world, in the most complete sense and a man of God, equally completely. . . . Perhaps it also explains how someone who was naturally drawn towards richness (of thought as well as of the good things of life) should have chosen the way of total poverty, especially of the spirit. He was not a man to accept the mediocre or shoddy in anything.

Of course Judith was not the first to observe this duality in John Main – the religious and the rascal, the seriousness with the humour. Father John's old friend from Trinity, Robert Farrell, analyses his sense of humour:

It is rather hard to describe his humour, jokes don't travel well in time and space. He had a highly developed sense of irony which seldom failed to express itself. He was a ruthless social critic. His sense of humour was part of his everyday conversation and he was always a fascinating companion. He certainly had his share of the Blarney – but it was not Blarney of the nudge and wink variety, oh dear no! It was ultra sophisticated Blarney that kept you wondering which of three possible meanings might be the correct one. It was very Irish in that it went from fact to fantasy and back again in the time it takes to swallow a mouthful of Guinness. I suspect that his sense of humour got him into a fair amount of trouble. It was misunderstood. If it was misunderstood, it could be resented as people didn't like games played on them. It certainly could be tiresome at times . . . and somebody once complained to me: 'You never know where you are at with that fellow, Main'.

I knew what they meant, but I understood Douglas and it never really bothered me. In part I think it was a way of defending himself in social situations that his reserve made painful for him.

Many years after the Trinity days, a lawyer friend of John Main's in Washington, Charles Emmett Lucey, observed this same mix of mischief and devoutness:

> He was often at my house at parties, with the boys, mixed and mingled, usually not in clerical garb, or if so, took off his Roman collar. Would drink Scotch, I think, never over-imbibed. Joined in. One night he took me to Baltimore. We got lost, stopped at a bar. We didn't care where we were. Had a couple of beers. (I did not count.) He was one of the guys. He was a deeply holy man but not a clerical. He imitated the gospel but wasn't always talking about it.

Then Charles Lucey described the other side:

> I went with my daughter-in-law to one of a series of morning lectures John Main was giving at St Anselm's. Years ago I had gone to Ronald Knox's Lenten sermons. This lecture of Father John's reminded me of those which I think is a high compliment. He articulated so well. He was a very special person. All the things he did and was interested in were things that had a dimension to them. Christianity was not a static thing with him – he moved with it – every part of the day. This included his social life. One drew from him that he believed in a deep and rich Christianity. Everyone he met was aware of this.

It is also true to say that many of those who met Father John only in his years in Montreal saw more of his serious and thoughtful, less of his humourous and waggish side. There is a natural explanation for this. Father John was under considerable pressure in the Montreal period: material pressure to keep the foundation viable; and mental pressure, with so little help, to keep its work developing. There was also a different kind of pressure from two groups of people. One, small, viewed him with some suspicion as a potential cult figure who was working some religious angle or other. The other group, somewhat larger and more dedicated, probably caused John Main more aggravation. These were the people who, much to his chagrin, tried to place him on a pedestal. He was the first to deprecate this kind of adulation. It was one of the reasons he wanted to keep his illness a private matter. Diana Ernaelsteen was aware how easily he could be misunderstood:

> I feel some find it hard to come to terms with those parts of Douglas that could have in another man grown into con-artist, charlatan or whatever you want to call it – but which he moulded into teacher, preacher with great goodness and charisma. I think it's a shock for those who knew Douglas in Montreal only to run into people who thought the whole thing was a sham. It wasn't. In him there was not only the most serious of people, but in paradox also the most unserious!

Indeed there were two sides to John Main, the serious and the unserious, the roguish and the reverent or, in more Irish terms, the magician and the mystic. Both sides were natural facets of the same person. As the years progressed both became more integrated and were transformed through meditation on the journey he was travelling. Though he never lost his humour nor his engaging charm, in Montreal he seemed more reflective, at times even sombre. This disappeared whenever he talked of meditation, with a bright urgency that was almost incandescent. Perhaps that is what a meditator in Dublin saw the last summer he was home: 'There seemed to be a certain brilliance about him, not only in mood but in aura.'

Father John spent one of his last days in Dublin with the family to whom he was so close. Then it was time to say goodbye – to say goodbye to his family, to the prayer groups, to Ireland. He turned to his sister, Yvonne, and said quietly, 'It would have been lovely to see Kerry again.' But there was no time. And for Father John there would never be time to see Kerry again.

After returning to Montreal he and Father Laurence went to Nova Scotia to give retreats. From there he wrote to an Ontario meditator in the first week of July:

> ... I am very much better and having returned from a lecture tour in England and Ireland, I am now giving a retreat in Nova Scotia. But next week I am going to take

two weeks of holiday – with absolutely nothing to do – with the Community in Iona, Nova Scotia.

Several members of the Montreal Community joined Father John and Father Laurence for two lovely weeks in a house loaned to them in Iona, a small village on the Bras d'Or Lakes. They meditated, took long walks to the seashore and enjoyed the beautiful scenery of Cape Breton. Father John, feeling remarkably well, read, wrote and, when the children in the group became importunate, played croquet and told them stories about his life. Polly Scofield's son made up plays in which everyone had a part. (Father John, with his stories and magic tricks, always had a special way with children.) They were happy sunny days by the sea. But they had to end. After the holidays on the way home, while stopping in Halifax to change aircraft, a knife's edge of pain cut through Father John. He was unable to complete a short walk through the Halifax airport.

After that experience, the pain, in varying degrees seldom left him again. On the night at the beginning of August when he returned to the Priory on Pine Avenue, the police appeared. There was an emergency with one of the Benedictine oblates, Don McGowan, a terminal patient at the Royal Victoria Hospital. Father John went to the hospital with Laurence to help give his friend the sacrament of the sick but he was too ill to go to the funeral. By now the pain was spreading. It had begun, like a sharp tooth-ache, in Father John's lower back and was now shooting down his right leg. Father John himself sometimes referred to his back problem as a slipped disc or an old war-wound. An orthopaedic surgeon, consulted at the Queen Elizabeth Hospital, thought the problem might be sciatica. X-rays showed no trauma in the lower back area. Now meditators and visitors who went to the Priory and who, up to this time had heard nothing of Father John's illness, were shocked to see him in a wheelchair.

Still, he carried on at the Priory in almost a normal fashion. A married couple from Montreal spent a week-end there in the latter part of August. Father John, briskly wheeling himself about, was in fine fettle. Nor was he upset (at least he did not show it) when the husband came within an ace of

177

destroying the large carpet outside Father John's room on the second floor of the Priory. The husband describes what happened:

After meditation and breakfast I looked around for some manual work. Could I clean the area just outside Father John's room? Indeed I could. There would be a cleaning machine waiting there for me. The machine looked to me like a carpet cleaner and when I plugged it in (underneath the picture of a bishop), it sounded like a carpet cleaner.

So naturally I pushed the cleaner onto the carpet. Then all hell broke loose. The machine began wrestling with the carpet. It bucked and weaved and dragged me across the carpet, chewing away as we went. I held on desperately like a water-skier behind a speedboat. At this juncture a member of the lay community appeared. He asked, with a look of horror, what I was doing. I explained I was trying to clean a carpet. He explained I was using a floor polisher.

Greatly relieved, I began to polish the floor around the carpet. Then Father John quietly opened his door and said, if I liked, to come in for a chat after I finished. There was nothing very memorable about our chat. I asked Father John if he thought I should change to another mantra. He didn't think so. Then I asked whether he thought my wife and I should try to start a meditation group in our home. He thought it was a great idea (and a month later we did).

During the rest of the week-end, we saw Father John around and about in his wheelchair. He had no hesitation about asking for a push. At recreation after supper sitting before the fireplace in the library he talked about Trinity and the law and the Irish government and a biography he was reading of a great nineteenth-century barrister. Except for the wheelchair you wouldn't have thought there was much wrong.

But there was a lot more wrong, and it was discovered indirectly. Radio-therapy had again been prescribed, this time directed to the lower back. And indeed by the end of August the pain in Father John's back had subsided. It had responded to the radio-therapy. This meant, although the X-rays had shown nothing, that the back problem was cancer.

It had now spread to the nerves in the lower spine. Yet, in some degree, Father John was feeling better and functioning better. In September he was spending more time out of the wheelchair, although his right leg was giving some trouble. One reason for the 'improvement' might relate to an addition to the medical team, Dr Balfour Mount. Dr Mount, a soft-spoken, caring man, was the founder of the Palliative Care Unit at the Royal Victoria Hospital, his attitude to the terminally ill much influenced by his close friendship with Dame Cicely Saunders and her pioneering work for the dying in Britain. Dr Mount is Canada's best-known specialist in pain control.

When he first spoke to Father John about his illness at the beginning of August, the only problem mentioned was the pain in his back. Dr Mount then referred Father John to a specialist, Dr Gilles Bertrand at the Montreal Neurological Institute. After seeing him, Dr Bertrand immediately called Dr Mount: 'You didn't tell me that Father Main has a chest malignancy.' Dr Mount was aghast. Father John had not told him about the chest cancer either. It is difficult to understand why Father John was so secretive with his doctors in this instance. Whatever the reason, Dr Mount was now on the medical team and would assist, when necessary, Dr Marcel Boisvert of the Royal Victoria's Palliative Care unit in Father John's home-care and pain control.

Although he was now spending more time in bed resting, Father John still gave the meditation talks twice weekly. He also continued to say the public Mass at 11 o'clock on Sunday, sometimes using his wheelchair, and delivering the homily, a little jewel that sparkled with fresh insight into the scriptural passage of the day. It was notable to watch John Main begin a talk on meditation or a homily. He would straighten up, close his eyes, then compress his shoulders as though he were plunging into some deep interior space.

All during August and September, Father John continued to see visitors at the Priory and to keep up his large correspondence. He wrote to a meditator in Ireland: 'Thank you for your letter . . . written from Kerry. How lovely to be in the Kingdom. I am sure it was a great inspiration for you. I never go home to Kerry without feeling a wonderful sense of spaciousness and freedom.'

The recipient of the letter wrote in the margin: 'As you probably know, Kerry is known as the Kingdom. Although the typist put a small 'k' you can see it was corrected to a capital. I can almost see him smiling as he wrote that.' Father John added a word about his health: 'The Lord has been telling me to be quiet, to be still and to be silent, and so I have spent some weeks lying very still while my back heals. I am glad to say it is getting better now.'

On the third Sunday in September, a glorious autumn day, the Montreal Community, including oblates and meditators from far and wide, celebrated the fifth anniversary of Father John's coming to Montreal to begin the foundation. The celebration at the Priory was a surprise for Father John. He was not in his wheelchair. He walked, very straight and a trifle slowly, out onto the stone patio overlooking Montreal lying in a golden haze. The sun shone through the brilliantly coloured leaves. The oblates and the meditators served cakes and tea. Father John chatted animatedly. He was enveloped by the warmth of the autumn sun and of those he loved and those who loved him.

It was a golden moment to remember. So much had been accomplished in so short a time. It was less than five years since Father John and Laurence had moved into the old Décarie House on Vendôme in December 1977. Father John had called it at the time 'a leap in the dark'. They had begun with a rickety house, Bishop Crowley's blessing, their own hopes and not much else. Now less than five years later there was this magnificent Priory on the wooded slopes of Mount Royal. There was a thriving meditation centre. And there were prayer groups, not only in Montreal and the rest of Canada and North America, but in many countries around the world. These were just the external manifestation of what Father John had begun. Beneath these, like subterranean springs, always bubbling to feed 'the work', was Father John's real and unique contribution.

John Main's contribution relates to three areas – prayer, monasticism and the laity – and their fresh relationship within John Main's vision. Prayer was central to his vision and, in a sense, the other elements – monasticism and the laity – depend on John Main's view of prayer and its place in daily life. In the area of prayer, John Main reintroduced the prayer phrase, the mantra (found in the Hindu tradition of the East and recovered from Cassian) into contemporary Western monasticism. In addition he made imageless prayer ('pure prayer') the basis for a fundamental shift in monastic priorities. His contribution here will only be seen in the perspective of time. But already there is evidence of a spirit of reform permeating parts of monastic life through John Main's emphasis that 'pure prayer' (and a serious daily commitment to it) forms the base of monastic mission and apostolate.

Finally, for John Main, prayer life led inevitably to community life. This notion of community, of 'fellowship', extended to lay communities as well, some composed of people living in the monastery (perhaps temporarily), others comprising people living in their own homes but participating in the life of the monastery and sharing their lives with each other in prayer groups, 'communities of faith' as Father John called them. For those living in the monastery John Main offered a unique blend of hospitality and distance revolving around the fellowship of the group and the silence and intensity of the prayer. That some who came were unable to realize fully this aspect of community in no way invalidates his 'vision'.

In summary, John Main's unique contributions are three: he rediscovered a formula, a discipline for 'pure', imageless prayer (and, in so doing, effected a further reconciliation between the prayer life of East and West); he provided in 'pure prayer' an instrument of reform for the monastic life, making the apostolate dependent on prayer, not the other way about; finally, he made 'pure', imageless prayer more accessible to the man in the street (as St Paul had always urged), and he made the man in the street more welcome to, and more integrated into, the prayer life of the monastery.

John Main's contribution, especially to the prayer life of modern man, should not be underestimated even after so little time. One of the world's leading teachers of prayer, Bede Griffiths, a Benedictine monk who has lived in ashrams in India for thirty years, says, 'In my experience John Main is the best spiritual guide in the Church today. I find something absolutely unique in him.' Bede Griffiths believes Father Main's teaching has wide appeal: 'The way he brings together, a precise method of meditation leading to contemplative prayer and community life based on love is exactly what we are seeking. . . .' And he adds, 'People are looking for just the kind of guidance in meditation which he gave. . . .'

Indeed John Main's contribution to prayer life, monastic life and the spiritual life of ordinary men and women is already substantial and influential. The extent of his influence is limited now only by time. As for John Main himself, he was, near the end, moving toward a more solitary kind of prayer life and monastic witness, delayed only by his failing health. Still, on that golden Sunday in September, five years after he had come, John Main's spirits were animated and joyful, despite his physical condition.

After the September day with the community, Father John was well enough to go to Cape Cod for a few days of rest with his Washington friends, Jack and Peg Davitt. After his return he wrote to Rosie Lovat on 6 October:

Thank you so much for all your inquiries about the doctor in Australia. I don't think there is very much more he could do for me but I will put it to my doctor who is an oncologist. In fact the two treatments that I have had on my chest and back were cobalt radiations – which is what they use here too.

On Friday I go for my X-ray to see if the chemotherapy has been working or not. I imagine it has.

In fact the X-ray taken two days later, revealed that Father John's chest cancer was much worse. Just two days before, he had given what was to be his last major public address. He spoke to 2,000 delegates of the International Seminar on Terminal Care. The talk was later published under the title, *Death: The Inner Journey*. Father Laurence Freeman writes in the Preface that the talk 'is a unique chapter in his teaching on meditation written and spoken during a time of physical suffering when the awareness of his own approaching death was growing daily sharper.' In this final major address Father John stressed, as he had so often, 'the inner journey':

The inner journey is a way of union. Firstly, it unites us to ourselves. Then (as our personal fulfilment is found beyond ourselves) it unites us to others. And then (as union with others opens up the heart of the mystery of love to us) it unites us with God, so that God may be all in all.

No one who knew John Main in the fall of 1982 could doubt he had travelled far on 'the inner journey'. Sister Camille Campbell of the Congregation of Notre Dame had come to the Priory in September to spend a year with Father John. Sister Camille sums up what she learned listening to Father John and helping him through his final months:

I began to understand that his teaching was leading me into what he called 'liberty of spirit'. Meditation is a way to that liberty, it gives us the freedom to take off our masks and simply be. It is a way of being free from the frustration of not being in contact with our inner selves. That is what I learned from listening to, watching and caring for Father John. As his illness grew more intense he grew more deeply into this freedom.

The day after his talk on death and the day before the serious X-ray showing the deterioration in his lungs, Father John wrote to Diana Ernaelsteen explaining why he had not written for a time:

I have had a slipped disc since August and have been quite incapacitated by it – a lot of discomfort and almost of despair that it would ever right itself again! But it is now much better and I can walk around without too much trouble. At the height – or depth – of it I was in a wheel-chair for about four weeks . . . !

I thought of you a lot when I was in Boston last week and driving down alongside the Charles River. I had just spent a week on Cape Cod – I thought the change would do me good, and get me out of my invalid way of thinking. It worked. I have been much better since.

Diana remembers Father John saying that he would die young. 'He was terrified of many things – like dying and flying.' But mainly 'he had a great hunger, to love others and to be loved':

> He is very deserving of that love in all his humanity and caring. He continued to grow and improve himself all his life as few others do. . . . I think you only need my contribution to understand the *meat*. The meat is the work, the really valid bit of Douglas' life. The bit he left behind integrated in others.

Although Diana believes that Father John was aware he was dying, there are no hints of it in the letters he continued to write. A meditator in Ireland wrote to say she would give up smoking while she visited Lourdes to help him regain his health. He replied:

> Thank you for your letter from Lourdes. Thank you too for your prayer and penance on my behalf. I hope you have kept off the smoking – it may well be the acceptable sacrifice that will bring me a cure! Thank you anyway for even hinting at it.

Another meditator from Dublin asked about changing her mantra. Father John answered:

> It is good to hear from you and to know that you keep faithful to the way of meditation. It is demanding but so worthwhile if you can only keep going. . . . I am so glad you enjoyed the visit during the summer. These little visits are terribly brief but it is very heartening for me to discover that you all keep faithful to the pilgrimage.

Characteristically, Father John said nothing in his reply about the woman's request to change her mantra. He believed the pilgrimage of prayer had certain fixed reference points and a stable mantra was one of them. Nor did his developing illness deprive him of his sense of humour. One night Father John fell out of bed. As Father Laurence helped him back, Laurence said, 'We'll laugh about this later.' Father John replied, 'Let's laugh about it now.' And they did. Nor was his Irish wit out of commission when he required it. A meditator from Ontario, obviously unaware of how ill Father John was, visited the Priory, then complained about everything from its intellectualism to the speedy recitation of the office. Father John thought this reaction a little too much and he responded in a letter dated October 15th:

I am sorry you found your stay so unrewarding and the liturgies so depressing. I don't think we set out to be very intellectual and I think in essence our message is one of very great simplicity. 'Say your Mantra.'

I am sorry that our Blessed Sacrament Chapel was not in operation for your visit. But it is so now. We have been a long time getting rid of the billiard table and so on. . . .

Perhaps I communicated the sombreness. If so my apologies. But while you were here I was in quite a bit of pain. Thank God it is now much better.

I am sorry the speed of the recitation [of the Office] was too much for you – at least this was not sombre! The Latin Compline I have always loved even when I could not understand the Latin.

Obviously John Main had lost none of his writing vigour.

At this time, mid-October, there were those in the Community who thought Father John would recover. Probably all of the Montreal meditators, still unaware of the medical situation, thought so too. A few days later he had a discussion about the whole situation with his oncologist, Dr Joan Zidulka. Dr Zidulka had the impression Father John was open to trying experimental therapy. But she was not: 'There comes a time, in my opinion, when further treatment is useless.' Dr Zidulka decided not to treat Father John's condition further. He explained this to Rosie:

I had a long consultation with my doctor today. She went with your letter to all the leading specialists around here and all agreed it would be senseless to go to Australia. As I think I told you I have had all the cobalt and radium treatment possible for my case. They are familiar with but not keen on the taking of the blood treatment. It is still in a very experimental stage and can make matters worse. So in the end they [other doctors] are putting me on a further course of treatment that is a little more severe than the first two but which they think I should be able to survive! The outlook is not very good but they are trying everything so hard.

There is no doubt that for almost seven months, since the 'hopeless' prognosis in early March, Father John had nurtured a hope of recovery, 'of beating it'. He had a history of resiliency, of bouncing back from less serious illnesses. But mainly it was a hope not shared by any of his medical team. It was a hope Father John himself had to summon every ounce of his courage and self-control to sustain. Moreover, as he told Dr Nancekivell, he did not want to cope with floods of pity and sympathy from outside friends and members of the Community itself. Later there were some people, good friends of Father John's, who felt the incomplete information about his illness was carried too far. So much so that many realized he had been seriously ill only when they heard, shockingly, that his illness had ended.

There was another reason, this one deeper, for maintaining the secrecy. Father John had a zest for life that was, in a sense, the obverse of his attitude to death. He had talked about this many years before with Diana Ernaelsteen. His father and grandfather had died at a relatively early age, so had his younger brother, Patrick. When Dr Nancekivell observed that 'he never manifested the slightest evidence of depression or ultimate fear', this was more a tribute to Father John's immense powers of self-control than it was to his lack of fear. Dr Balfour Mount, monitoring the pain level, noted this incredible self-control; one reason it was so difficult to gauge how much pain Father John was suffering was because he so seldom complained about it. But Dr Mount also judged that beneath the self-control there was a major struggle going on within John Main, not so much a physical struggle as a struggle on the spiritual and psychological plane.

One can merely speculate on the nature of that struggle. But it was surely part of his journey and, could it not be suggested, a fearful part, the last darkness before the light. The struggle was an understandable reflection of his natural fear of death. The struggle was a symptom of how much he still wanted to live for human reasons, to see his family again, and Ireland and all his friends. The struggle was also a sign of how much there remained to do, to put the Montreal foundation on a solid base, to develop the teaching on Christian meditation, to prepare Laurence to carry on the 'work' of the pilgrimage. Why had he been given so critical a task for the community, the Church, the world? And why was he given so little time to see it through? Is it surprising he was puzzled at first and only fully realized later, nearer the end, how essential this portion of his journey was and that it must be travelled, for the most part, in faith and alone. With this realization he began to let go, even of those things that seemed to be important, as he had let go so many times in meditation.

It is not invalid to speculate that these were some of the elements of the struggle within, a titanic struggle because John Main was a big man with a big heart and a big task. He continued the struggle through October and November. What Dr Nancekivell saw then was 'a lion of a man buoyed up by his profound faith'. What nurse Sue Britton saw later in December was 'a man letting go and moving deeply into the experience of his own dying'. The radio-therapy treatments he was still undergoing relieved the pain but weakened him.

Still, in the early autumn in the weekly talks he gave to the meditators, there were only minor manifestations of the illness and the struggle. Father John limped slightly and sat a little more stiffly. His rich voice was a little thin, a little tired. A great energy was summoned from a great depth to complete the talk with clarity, vitality, even humour. During one of his last talks to the meditation group, about mid-November, he said, 'When the call comes it is absolutely unmistakable.' The call to which he was referring was not the call of death. It was the call to love.

On the evening of November 10th despite the pain, Father John travelled to the outskirts of Montreal to the Villa Marguerite of the Congregation of Notre Dame, to talk to several oblate and meditation groups. It was his last public meeting outside the Priory. The next day, Friday, there was a special event at the Priory, one which Father John had been eagerly anticipating, a celebration of the work of various artists – poets, sculptors, writers, musicians – and how meditation moulded and changed their work. Father John was present for the opening talks on the Friday night. He also came down for the Saturday morning discussion. He remained for lunch, friendly, chatting, looking pale and tired. That was the last time he came downstairs for a community meal. At one point during the Arts week-end, a Montreal meditator inquired about his back, then asked, 'Do you have a doctor?' His face lit up and he replied, 'The very best in the world.' Another treatment in radio-therapy seemed to break his strength.

About this time, in the early days of December, Father John fully accepted the medical consequences of his condition. He told Dr Nancekivell, 'I have abandoned wild hopes and I accept the future.' He still got up to eat and to write letters in his room until 12 December. He knew all his old friends at Ealing were praying with him and that Abbot Rossiter had offered to fly him to London for further treatment. His own bishop, Leonard Crowley, who had helped so much at the beginning, was near his friend at the end and later the Bishop would write: 'Dom Main's singleness of vision was a source of inspiration for extraordinary numbers of people who came to the Benedictine house to meditate, to grow and to become prayerful people.' Father John's last Newsletter from the Montreal Priory, dated 8 December, dealt with prayer and the Christmas Mystery:

The mystery surrounding Jesus was perceptible from the beginning of his life. Not until his death and resurrection was it capable of being fully apprehended, fully known. Because not until then was it complete. Our life does not achieve full unity until it transcends itself and all limitation by passing through death.

Father John's passage was beginning. The glowing pain was burning away the base of his spine. Had he lived he would have been paralyzed. But even as he began to die, his life's work continued. A meditator in London had written to Sister Madeleine Simon, Father John's friend in London: 'John's talk last night [on tape] reminded me so much of Eliot's Four Quartets, particularly the following stanzas from "East Coker" ' . . .

I said to my soul, be still, and wait without hope
For hope would be hope for the wrong thing; wait without
  love
For love would be love of the wrong thing; there is yet
  faith
But the faith and the love and the hope are all in the
  waiting.
Wait without thought, for you are not ready for thought:
So the darkness shall be the light, and the stillness the
  dancing.

Eliot's words describe many aspects of the silent imageless prayer that John Main rediscovered in John Cassian by way of the Malayan swami and passed on to the Christian Church he loved. The words could also describe the Priory at the Christmas of Father John's dying, glowing with the warmth of the fireplace and the love of the community singing the carols of peace in the flickering candlelight.

In the last days many from the community gathered outside Father John's room to say the Benedictine Office and to meditate in silence. Father Laurence (who had nursed him faithfully and lovingly for weeks), Brother Paul Geraghty and others of the Montreal meditators remained by his side hour after hour. Father John's own breathing, scarcely laboured, radiated a sense of presence and peace. About 8.45 o'clock on the morning of 30 December, in the Priory he had founded, surrounded by those he loved and whom he had guided on the pilgrimage, Father John's life achieved its full unity by passing through death. In the darkness there was light and in the stillness, dancing.

Epilogue

Since Father John's death about four years ago, 'the work' he began in Montreal has been, to use his own words, 'on the move'. In Montreal itself, under Father John's successor as Prior, Father Laurence Freeman, the monastic community has thrived. Paul Geraghty OSB became a priest in 1986. Several young men are now in various stages of their Benedictine training. Others are considering the monastic life. Still others, part of the lay community, live at the Priory and go out to their work in hospitals and elsewhere. Many guests come to stay and pray for different periods.

One of the most exciting developments, always part of Father John's vision, was the opening of a women's residence, just down the street from the Priory. The residence, with about half-a-dozen women, is associated with a Benedictine Convent in Minnesota. Another house of rest and retreat for the community, 'Lumen Christi', is being developed at Benson, Vermont, under the direction of Dom Gerald Regis OSB, also a member of the Montreal Priory.

Of course the expansion of 'the work' is not restricted to Montreal. Father Laurence has travelled extensively to encourage the growing number of oblates and prayer groups. Meditation centres are being established in London, Melbourne, New York City, Boston and at Berkeley in California. Father Laurence also visited the monastic complex in Kuala Lumpur where Father John learned to meditate with Swami Satyananda and spoke with the late Swami's assistant, a Hindu nun, Sister Mangalam.

Father John's words are still going out from the Priory in publications and cassettes. At the end of 1985 his final book, *The Present Christ*, was published. (Father Laurence's first book, *Light Within,* was published in 1986.) Father John's books are gradually being translated into other languages, such as French, German and Portuguese. The Communitas Tapes, talks given by Father John, are also going out to meditators and the groups he called 'communities of faith' all over the world. Each summer the 'John Main Seminar' is held at the Priory, its general purpose being to examine the relationship between Christian meditation and daily life as it is manifested in philosophy, literature and the arts.

The realization that so many people of all backgrounds have begun the pilgrimage of Christian meditation has led to the launching of 'Unitas', a forum for meditators developed by meditators and published by the Montreal Priory. In addition an Animators' week-end for leaders of meditation groups was held in Montreal in the autumn of 1985. Participants came from several countries. Another is planned for 1987 and similar get-togethers for animators have taken place in England and elsewhere. A series of talks on meditation, designed for the workplace, was given on the site to employees of Alcan, one of Canada's leading industrial companies.

It is remarkable how 'the work' begun by Father John has flowered so quickly under the steady direction of his successor, Father Laurence. As before, at the centre of 'the work' is the prayer. And from the prayer flows all the rest.

Notes on Sources

Most of John Main's letters cited in the biography were made available to me by the following: Jane Akers-Jones; the Benedictine Priory of Montreal; Dr Diana Ernaelsteen (Searle); Michael Hall OSB; and Lady Lovat. The immediate members of Father John's family provided information on many aspects of his life particularly his early years. These family members included especially his sister, Yvonne Fitzgerald. Also his other sisters and brother, Diane O'Neill (and her husband Hugh), Kitty Stanley and Ian Main (and his wife, Judith, for her moving memoir).

Father Laurence Freeman OSB, Father John's successor as Prior, was most helpful in providing insights and in reviewing the material for accuracy especially for the Montreal period. However, errors of fact or judgement in the book are mine. Most of the other material in the biography was obtained by interviews with friends and associates of John Main in his military, academic, colonial and monastic careers. For the most part, these interviews took place in Dublin, London, Montreal and Washington.

A final source of information includes books, other publications, records and cassettes written and recorded by John Main and others.

INTRODUCTION

Most of the material comes from the following publications by John Main:

Main, John, *Christian Meditation: The Gethsemani Talks*. Montreal: The Benedictine Priory, 1977.

——, *Letters from the Heart*. New York: Crossroad, 1982.

——, *Moment of Christ*. London: Darton, Longman and Todd, 1984, New York: Crossroad, 1984.

——, *The Monastic Adventure*. Montreal: The Benedictine Priory, 1983.

——, *Monastic Prayer and Modern Man*. Montreal: The Benedictine Priory, 1983.

——, *The Present Christ*. London: Darton, Longman and Todd, 1985, New York: Crossroad, 1985.

——, *Word into Silence*. London: Darton, Longman and Todd, 1980. New York: Paulist Press, 1981.

Mott, Michael, *The Seven Mountains of Thomas Merton*. Boston: Houghton, Mifflin Company, 1984, pp. 528, 433.

CHAPTER 1: BEGINNINGS IN BALLINSKELLIGS

I am indebted to members of the Main family and to other relatives and friends of John Main.

Interviews: Eileen Beck; John Boland; Dr Mary Ellen Bradshaw; Molly Curran; Nora Curtin; Margaret Dodd; Yvonne Fitzgerald; John Foll; Ian Main; Diane O'Neill; Daid O'Sullivan; Kitty Stanley.

Publications:

Comerford, R. W., *A Study in Irish Nationalism and Literature*. Port Marnock: Wolfhound Press, 1979.

CHAPTER 2: FROM CIRCUS MASTER TO THE JESUITS

Most of the material was provided by the Main family, former teachers, fellow students and Dr Diana Ernaelsteen.

Interviews: Sister Anthony; Eileen Beck; Guy Brinkworth SJ; Nora Curtin; Margaret Dodd; Dr Diana Ernaelsteen; Mr Henley; Hugh Kay; Marie Main; Martin Miller; Grace Ward; Peggy Winser.

Letters: Peter Hannegan; Peter Hirst; Paul Kennedy SJ; Madeleine Simon RSCJ.

Publications:

Barrington, T. J., *Discovering Kerry*. Dublin: The Blackwater Press, 1976.

Busby, Richard, *The Book of Welwyn*. Buckingham: Barracuda Books, 1976.

CHAPTER 3: SPECIAL COMMUNICATIONS UNIT NO. 4

I am especially indebted to the late The Rt Hon. Sir Hugh Fraser MBE, who helped me obtain information on John Main's military record through the British Ministry of Defence. I also wish to acknowledge the help of S. C. Routh and M. E. Hawes of that Ministry. Much of the material in this chapter comes from information contained in John Main's 'Soldier's Service and Pay Book';

also from interviews and letters with those associated with John Main in the Second World War, especially his good friends, Harry Spendiff and Tudor Jones.

Most of the material on John Main's journalistic career comes from members of his family and from the records and staff of the *Hornsey Journal*, and William Harris (former editor).

Military career:
Interviews: Dick Cartwright; Tudor Jones; Ian Main; Harry Spendiff; Eddie Williams.
Letters: Major A. G. Harfield (Royal Signals Museum);
M. E. Hawes (Ministry of Defence); Harry Spendiff; Eddie Williams.
Publications:
Hinsley, F. H., *British Intelligence in the Second World War*. Cambridge: 1979 (volumes 1 and 2).
Lewin, Ronald, *Ultra Goes to War*. London: Hutchinson, 1978.
Winterbotham, F. W., *The Ultra Secret*. New York: Dell, 1974.

CHAPTER 4: THE CANONS, DUBLIN AND THE LAW

Much of the material is from associates of John Main in the Canons Regular of the Lateran and also at Trinity College, Dublin. I am especially grateful for the assistance of E. Y. 'Don' Exshaw, Professor of Law at Trinity. Robert Farrell, a student with John Main at Trinity, provided me with one of the most sensitive and insightful reminiscences of his friend that I have read.

Canons Regular of the Lateran:
Interviews: Laurence Byrne CRL; Father Dunstan CRL; Brocard Sewell O. CARM.; Charles White CRL; Father Whitehead CRL; Albert Wyatt CRL.
Letters: Vincent Pugliese CRL.
Publications and Records:
McDonald, Most Rev. W. J. (ed.), *New Catholic Encyclopedia*. New York: McGraw-Hill, 1967, pp. 62–4.
'Libellus Studiorum' Douglas Main, Faculty of Theology, Angelicum University, Rome, 1949–50.
Eileen Main, Diary, 1946.

Trinity College (student 1950–4):
Interviews: John Boland; Prof. Frank E. Dowrick; Prof. E. Y. Exshaw; Patrick Raftery.
Letters: Connie Critchley; Robert Farrell; Hugh O'Neill; Dermod D. Owen-Flood QC.

Publications:
Calendar, Trinity College, Dublin, 1984–85.

CHAPTER 5: MALAYA AND THE SWAMI

Much of the material comes from associates of John Main who were in Malaya in the mid-1950s in Her Majesty's Oversea Civil Service. For the most part, the material on Swami Satyananda was derived from written sources.

Interviews: Kenneth P. Cleary; Bernard L. Drake; Philip Egerton.

Letters: Jane Akers-Jones; Robert Bruce; Robert Farrell; A. W. D. James; Timothy Raison (Overseas Development Administration): J. H. A. Scarlett; Thomas Schlafly; T. E. Smith; C. K. E. Tung.

Publications:

Baker, Noel, *The War of the Running Dogs*. London: Collins, 1971.

Main, John, *Christian Meditation*.

McKie, Ronald, *The Emergence of Malaya*. New York: Harcourt, Brace & World, Inc., 1963, p. 11.

Nair, V. G., *Swami Satyananda and Cultural Relations Between India and Malaya*. Kuala Lumpur: The Pure Life Society, 1960.

The Pure Life Society, 'Annual Report and Accounts for 1954'. Kuala Lumpur

——, 'Silver Jubilee Magazine, 1949–74'. Kuala Lumpur: 1975.

CHAPTER 6: DINNERS IN LONDON

The chief sources are John Main's family, Dr Diana Ernaelsteen, and John Main's associates (professors and students) at Trinity College. Again I want to mention Professor E. Y. Exshaw for his assistance in locating people and records. John Boland, Father Main's fellow-student and long-time friend was also helpful.

Interviews: Robert Ernest Blakney; John Boland; Heather Colquhoun; Connie Critchley; Michael Dickson; Prof. Frank E. Dowrick; Dr Diana Ernaelsteen; Prof. E. Y. Exshaw; Robert Farrell; Graham Golding; Mary Lodge Jennings; Daid O'Sullivan; Patrick Raftery; Prof. Edward Stuart.

Letters: Dr Diana Ernaelsteen; Robert Farrell; Garret Fitzgerald, TD; Hugh O'Neill; Dermod D. Owen-Flood, QC.

Publications:

Main, *Christian Meditation*.

CHAPTER 7: BECOMING A MONK

Most of the material derives from a series of interviews with the monks of Ealing. I am grateful to Bernard Orchard OSB for helping to arrange these:

Interviews: Vincent Cooper OSB: Connie Critchley; Nora Curtin; Anthony Gee OSB; Isabelle Glover; Catherine Hay; Benedict O'Donohue OSB; Bernard Orchard OSB; David Pearse OSB; Gilbert Smith OSB; Dunstan Watkins OSB.

Letters: Aidan Bellinger OSB; John Boland; John Foll; Rev. Gregory Meere; Rt Rev. Timothy Sweeney OSB.

Publications and Records:

Main, *Christian Meditation*.

'Libellus Studiorum, 1960–63, of John Main, Faculty of Theology, S. Anselmo, Rome.

CHAPTER 8: DISCOVERY IN WASHINGTON

Most of the material comes from Father John's associates at St Anselm's Abbey School in Washington, DC. I am especially grateful for the assistance of John Farrelly OSB and Michael Hall OSB.

Interviews: Alban Boultwood OSB; William Colby; Jack and Peggy Davitt; John Farrelly OSB; Michael Hall OSB; John and Bonnie Hardy; Charles Emmet Lucey; Bernard Marthaler OFM Conv; Aidan Shea OSB; Victor Thuroney; Aileen Winkopp.

Letters: Eltin Griffin O. CARM.

Publications:

Davitt, Jack, 'Schanachie', *Monastic Studies*, Advent, 1984, p. 39.

Main, John 'The View', *Review for Religious*, vol. 29, no. 3, May 1970, p. 360–3.

——, 'Talks to Nuns at Pinner', Cassettes, 1979.

CHAPTER 9: LONDON: THE FIRST MEDITATION CENTRE

I am especially grateful to some of those who were members of the first lay community at Ealing, such as Tom Abraham, Pat Hawes and Nicholas Wardropper. Also to Father John's successor at the first Meditation Centre, Benedict O'Donohue OSB. Material on the abbatial elections is based on letters and interviews with Father John's associates.

Interviews: Tom Abraham; John Boland; Eileen Byrne; Dr Walter M. Elsasser; John Farrelly OSB; Catherine Hayes; Pat Hawes; Benedict O'Donohue OSB; Bernard Orchard OSB; Miriam O. Quigley MMM; Tom Schlafly; Nicholas Wardropper.

Publications:
Main, *Letters from the Heart*. New York: Crossroad, 1982.
——, *Christian Meditation*.
Schaff, P. and Wace, H. (eds.), *The Nicene and Post-Nicene Fathers*, vol. XI, part 3, 'The Twelve Books of John Cassian', pp. 404–8.
Main, John. Cassette of Wimbledon Retreat. Summer 1977, 'Awakening Tapes'.

CHAPTER 10: GOODBYE TO EALING

The most significant material was derived from letters made available to me by Michael Hall OSB. Other material comes from Father John's associates at Ealing and St Anselm's who have been cited in previous chapters.
Interviews: Benedictines associated with Father John at Ealing and St Anselm's; John Boland; Eileen Byrne; Isabelle Glover; Father Bob Harris; Hans Kruitwagen; Miriam O. Quigley MMM.
Publications and Records:
Main. *Letters from the Heart*.
——, *Christian Meditation*.
Mott, Michael. *The Seven Mountains of Thomas Merton*. Boston: Houghton, Mifflin, 1984, pp. 301, 277, 423, 282, 320, 528, 543, 545, 433, 452.
Crowley, Bishop Leonard. 'A Monk of Vision', *Monastic Studies*, Advent, 1984, p. 49.
Main, John, Cassettes of Wimbledon 'Awakening' Retreat, Summer 1977.
'Benedictine File'. Chancery Office, Archdiocese of Montreal.

CHAPTER 11: BEGINNING IN MONTREAL

Much of the information comes from Laurence Freeman OSB and from those associated in some capacity with the community, first at Vendôme and later at Pine Avenue.
Interviews: Tom Abraham; Eileen Byrne; Laurence Freeman OSB; Paul Geraghty OSB; Pat Hawes; Paul Lafontaine; David Laing: Kit Laing; Robert Lemire; Dr Arthur Nancekivell; Myrtle Neel; Jean Prieur; Nicholas Wardropper.
Publications and Records:
Main, *Letters from the Heart*
'Benedictine File.' Chancery Office, Archdiocese of Montreal.

CHAPTER 12: THE LEADER AND THE LED

Much of the material comes from those already cited in interviews relating to Father John's periods at Ealing and St Anselm's. Here I list only those who made additional information available.

Interviews: Tom Abraham; Brenda Bury; Eileen Byrne; Camille Campbell CND; Elizabeth Egan; John Farrelly OSB; Andrew and Marie Foley; Laurence Freeman OSB; Isabelle Glover; Michael Hall OSB; Pat Hawes; Paul Lafontaine; Aidan Shea OSB; Madeleine Simon RSCJ.

Letters: Bede Griffiths OSB; Paul McDonald OSB.

Publications:

Du Boulay, Shirley, *Cicely Saunders: The Founder of the Modern Hospice Movement*. London: Hodder and Stoughton, 1984, p. 135.

Mott, *The Seven Mountains of Thomas Merton*, p. 452.

CHAPTER 13: THE TEACHER AND THE TEACHING

I am especially indebted to Andrew Foley, philosopher, meditator and writer in Boston, for his rich insights into the dynamics of Christian meditation. Also to his wife, Marie, for her perceptive observations on Father John's teaching. I have also relied in this and other chapters on a warm and expressive memoir of Father John by a Dublin meditator, Lucy MacDonald.

Interviews: Andrew and Marie Foley; Paul Lafontaine.

Letters: Father John Smith.

Publications and Records:

Dehqani-Tafti, H. B. (Bishop in Iran), *The Hard Awakening*. London: Triangle Books, 1981, pp. 101–2.

Main. See under Introduction, p. 000.

Pennington, M. Basil, *Centering Prayer*. Garden City: Image Books, 1982.

Y. D. 'Pour célébrer l'infinité de Dieu', *L'Église de Montréal*, no. 42, 13 Nov. 1980.

Campbell, Camille CND, 'A Man for Others', *Monastic Studies*, Advent 1984, p. 65.

Schumacher, E. F., *Small is Beautiful*. London: Blond & Briggs, 1973.

Freeman, Laurence OSB, 'Newsletter from the Benedictine Priory', 3 Sept. 1985.

Anonymous memoir of an Irish meditator, 'A Sort of Letter from the Heart', unpublished, 31 Oct. 1983.

Main, John, Cassettes of the Pinner Retreat, 1979.

——, Cassettes of the Toronto Talks, Nov. 9, 1980.

CHAPTER 14: THE END OF THE BEGINNING

Most of the material relating to his illness and death was obtained from Father John's doctors and other medical personnel. I was at the Priory the day before he died and spent most of the time in his bedroom. I am also indebted in this final chapter to Father John's sister-in-law, Judith Main, for her short memoir, first written in 1983, entitled 'Impressions of Dom John Main OSB, later published in *Monastic Studies*. Her impressions are very perceptive and moving.

Interviews: Martin Boler OSB; Sue Britton RN; Dr Marcel Boisvert; Camille Campbell CND; Dr Diana Ernaelsteen; Laurence Freeman OSB; Dr Balfour Mount; Dr Arthur Nancekivell; Linda Redpath; Polly Scofield; Dr Joan Zidulka.

Letters: Dr Diana Ernaelsteen; Peter Day; Robert Farrell; Charles Emmet Lucey; Hugh O'Neill; Margaret Roberts RSCJ.

Publications:

Eliot, T. S., 'East Coker', *Four Quartets*, London: Faber and Faber, 1944, p. 19. Quoted by permission of the publishers.

Campbell, Camille CND, 'A Man for Others', *Monastic Studies*, Advent, 1984, p. 49.

Crowley, Bishop Leonard, 'A Monk of Vision', *Monastic Studies*, Advent 1984, p. 49.

Main, John, 'Newsletter from the Priory', 8 Dec. 1982.

Main, Judith, 'Impressions of Dom John Main OSB' 1983.

Freeman, Laurence OSB, 'John Main's Obituary', *The Tablet*, London, 15 Jan. 1983.

Writings of John Main

Word into Silence (London, Darton, Longman and Todd, 1980; New York, Paulist Press, 1981)
Letters from the Heart (New York, Crossroad, 1982)
Moment of Christ (London, Darton, Longman and Todd, 1984; New York, Crossroad, 1984)
The Present Christ (London, Darton, Longman and Todd, 1985; New York, Crossroad, 1985)

Published by the Benedictine Priory of Montreal (also available from the Christian Meditation Centre, London):

Christian Meditation: The Gethsemani Talks (1977)
Christian Mysteries: Prayer and Sacrament (1979)
Death: The Inner Journey (1983)
The Hunger for Prayer (1983)
The Monastic Adventure (1983)
Monastic Prayer and Modern Man (1983)
The Other-Centeredness of Mary (1983)
Community of Love (1984)

Monastic Studies (1984) no. 15, devoted to the life and work of John Main, and the *Communitas* tapes by John Main are available from the Christian Meditation Centre, London, and the Benedictine Priory, Montreal. Addresses:

Christian Meditation Centre
29 Campden Hill Road
London W8 7DX
England
Tel: 01 937 0014

The Benedictine Priory
1475 Pine Avenue West
Montreal H3G 1B3
Canada
Tel: 514 849 2728

Index

201

John XXIII, Pope 67
Jones, Tudor 34–5
Joyce, James 4, 58
Jung, Carl 106

Kennedy, Fr Paul, sj 30, 37–8
Kickham, Charles J. 17
Knox, Mgr Ronald 175
Kruitwagen, Hans and
  Margaret 70, 95–7

Lafontaine, Paul 117, 138–9,
  145, 163
Laing, David 125–6
Laing, Mrs Peter (Kit) 125–6
Law, Dr 98
Lévesque, René 96
Lonergan, Fr Bernard, sj 8
Long, Fr Launcelot 26
Lovat, Lady: 83; character 109;
  meditation group 115–16;
  oblate 119; letters from J. M.
  110, 111, 120, 121, 123–31,
  148, 165, 169
Lovat, Lord 83
Lucey, Charles Emmet 175

MacDonald, Dom Paul, osb
  135–6, 140
Main, Allan Patrick (brother)
  18, 54, 67, 78, 186
Main, David Patrick
  (grandfather) 16–17
Main, David (nephew) 62–3
Main, David Patrick (father):
  birth and work 16; marriage
  17; character and personality
  18–21, 26, 29, war-time
  duties 32, 36; retirement 39;
  death 68, 119
Main, Diane *see* O'Neill, Diane
Main, Eileen Hurley (mother):
  birth 17; education, nursing
  career and marriage 17: faith

and personality 20–1, 23, 26;
  war-time duties 32; diary 37;
  illness and death 76–7
Main, Ethel *see* O'Shea, Ethel
Main, Ian (brother) 18, 21–2,
  25, 27
Main, Dom John (Douglas),
  osb (1926–82): birth and
  baptism 18; childhood and
  religious influences 21–2
  Education (1931–42): St
  Mary's, Hendon 23–4;
  Ballinskelligs national school
  24–5; first Communion 25;
  Highgate Junior School 25;
  Westminster Choir school
  25–7; St Ignatius College
  27–30
  Journalist (1942–3): *Hornsey
  Journal* 31
  Royal Corps of Signals (1943–6):
  enlistment and training
  32–3; European posting and
  intelligence operations 33,
  34; move to Germany and
  discharge 35
  *Canons Regular of the Lateran
  (1946–50)*: history 37;
  experience with 37–9
  Law Student (1950–4): enters
  Trinity, academic and social
  life 40–2; spiritual
  development and views 42–4
  *British Oversea Civil Service
  (1954–6)*: acceptance and
  studies, social life 45–8;
  meets Hindu Swami 49–52;
  retirement from service and
  views of policy 52–3
  Teacher of Law (1956–9):
  appointment and teaching
  methods 54; politics,
  scholarship, social life 55–7;